Tanea Hill is an author and a songwriter who has been writing for over 10 years. Over her 40-year time span, she has produced dance electronic and hip-hop music on iTunes and YouTube called *More Fun in Milan*, *Music and Catwalk (Remix)*, and *Plaid T-Shirt*. Tanea has also written amateur books. She is now working on her first professional book *Pyjama Stories*.

Dedicated to my friends, my family and my loving cousin Lil Ricky who passed away from a rare cancer Gamma Delta. I love you all and without your support, this book would never be possible. Thank you.

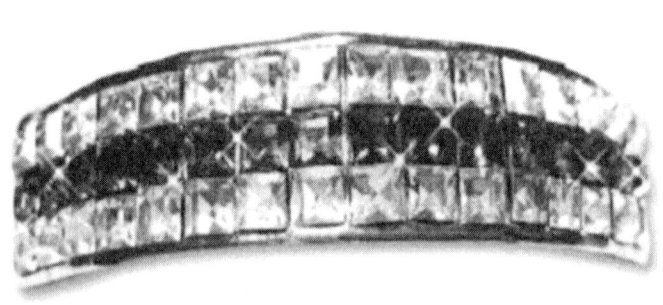
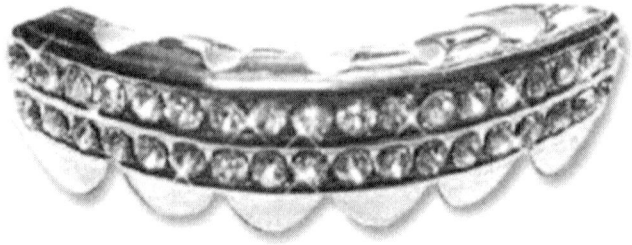

Tanea Hill

# PAJAMA STORIES: VOLUME 2

The Lady DJ and the Secret Society of 31 Platinum Grills

AUSTIN MACAULEY PUBLISHERS™
LONDON • CAMBRIDGE • NEW YORK • SHARJAH

Copyright © Tanea Hill (2021)

The right of Tanea Hill to be identified as author of this work has been asserted by the author in accordance with section 77 and 78 of the Copyright, Designs and Patents Act 1988.

All rights reserved. No part of this publication may be reproduced, stored in a retrieval system, or transmitted in any form or by any means, electronic, mechanical, photocopying, recording, or otherwise, without the prior permission of the publishers.

Any person who commits any unauthorised act in relation to this publication may be liable to criminal prosecution and civil claims for damages.

This is a work of fiction. Names, characters, businesses, places, events, locales, and incidents are either the products of the author's imagination or used in a fictitious manner. Any resemblance to actual persons, living or dead, or actual events is purely coincidental.

A CIP catalogue record for this title is available from the British Library.

ISBN 9781528934954 (Paperback)
ISBN 9781528968089 (ePub e-book)

www.austinmacauley.com

First Published (2021)
Austin Macauley Publishers Ltd
25 Canada Square
Canary Wharf
London
E14 5LQ

Brooklyn College Sociology Department for teaching me about race, class and gender. For teaching me that every occupation is meaningful no matter how poor class it may seem. Every job position in the world matters. Eddy Nunez, my music producer, who has stuck by through thick and thin. My Auntie Glynda who never turned her back on me no matter how hard things got. And my friends and family who stuck by me when I took chances.

# Chapter 1

Providence admired her new blue diamond-filled, platinum grill mouthpiece fronts that she had received from a group known as 31 Platinum Grills. She had become a member of the group before her graduation from the academy of DJs in New York City. Out of all the platinum fronts that she had exchanged and received, Jose, one of her group members, had taken a perfect impression of her teeth and had designed one of the most attractive platinum grill fronts that she had ever seen. Providence had been sworn into a secret society known as 31 Platinum Grills that had been founded four years earlier by some amateur DJs attending a small university known as the Academy of DJs. The organisation had been designed and developed for amateur DJs who had superb and unique skills.

They were given the keys to the city unlocking some of the most prestigious events and premiers that a DJ could host. Providence admired her freshly studded eyelids with rhinestones that sat at the very bottom of her eyelashes. She was pleased at how well they stayed on her eyelids without a bunch of eye glue. She prepared for her performance at the international hair show. Tonight she would be better known as DJ Lady Lucina to the crowd of people, she thought, as she checked her hairpiece and her streaked colourful tracks that her favourite beautician had sewn in. Her hair had been shaved on the sides with her stage name engraved that read "Lady" on one side and "Lou" on the other side. Tonight she would be meeting the first founder of the secret society of 31 Platinum Grills, named DJ Calm, who had given her very first job placement. She slipped into her tailor-made one-piece Brahmin suit that she purchased in New York City. The suit was accented and layered with ostrich feathers and colourful crocodile skins that fit every curve of her body. The suit had come with a matching clutch purse, and matching high heels. She checked her underarms to make sure her deodorant hadn't smeared on her expensive clothing, as she admired her 5-foot 8 racehorse body. Her skin was a reddish tone, which accented her light freckles. She had inherited her reddish-brown hair and freckles from her great grandmother who was an Irish servant from England during the early 1900s. Although she appeared to be an African American redbone, her features insisted that she was mixed with Scottish and Irish. Her grandmother had passed down her glowing skin tone, and now she had managed so well to maintain it using expensive skin products and Neutrogena. Her lip-gloss was clear and thick with a deep fuchsia blush that accented her amber bronze eyes. Providence's inspiration to pursue a career in the D' Jing industry had come from her yearly summer visits to Detroit. From since she was thirteen, Detroit's blocks were filled with African American men, women, gays, and transgender, who flaunted hair weaves, ponytails, up do's, stylish freeze curls, finger waves, haircuts, and slanted bangs. Detroit's streets were filled with candy paint cutlasses, with pickle juice greens, sparkly grape fuchsias, and tangerine oranges complimented with white leather interiors, that could be spotted through sparkly window tint on custom wheels with loud sound systems humping and bumping Detroit's most native booty bouncing music. Providence had easily adapted to Detroit's native music and had created and recorded music using similar native beats with cartoonist vocalists.

Providence prepared herself for channel 7's interview at the international hair show. A host named Shaw would be coaching DJ Calm and her before the interview. Shaw was a known popular hair model from NYC Hair Magazine whose nationality was mixed, with Sicilian, Arabian, and African American… She was tall and thin with long, thick, coarse hair that was perfect for a stylist. She had been working for a hairdresser from Sicily who had helped to increase her popularity and prestige, and so far, her popularity was soaring across New York.

Providence reviewed the program pamphlet that Shaw had given her. She was 3rd on the list and would be hosting the main event following DJ Calm who would be hosting the BYOB event. Providence smiled at the thought of mingling for the rest of the night as she remembered to grab her signature list and training program. Tonight she would put on her freshest face as she walked through the party making inquiries and gathering job leads with her signature list full of telephone numbers. Providence adjusted the blinds in her living room. It was a beautiful summer day in New York City. She loaded her DJ equipment and waited by the door for her escort, DJ Calm, to arrive from 31 Platinum Grills. As one of the first founders of 31 Platinum Grills, Calm had secured his position in the secret society as a trainer for amateur DJs. Tonight he would be escorting and meeting the infamous

Lady Lucina for the first time. The two would be taking a ride, sightseeing through Queens Astoria, enjoying the view of mansion style homes, soft textured lawns, and driveways filled with Lamborghinis, Porsches, Corvettes, Rolls Royces, Bentleys, Ferraris, and Benzes. Calm had planned to make dinner reservations at one of his favourite restaurants in Queens before the event. He arrived in a 2012 Cadillac truck on chrome wheels. He was 5'10" with a medium muscular build. His honey brown skin, deep waves, and gigantic, thick, pink lips, gave Providence an instant arousal when she looked at him. Calm's eyes were low and innocent and his voice was charming with a New York accent that resembled Wu Tang speech. During the ride, the two exchanged serious sex faces, as they listened to the Aaliyah song 'Let Me know'. Calm explained the ropes about the process of DJ'ing. Always have an extra pair of headphones sound proof to focus strictly on the music. Make sure all water containers are sealed and your CDs have top sticky labels that are visible in a plastic colourful case. Make sure all cords are smooth dry and untangled. Make sure all cases have plastic handles and steel boxes. Providence admired Calm during their intellectual conversation. He was wearing a black Prada fisherman's hat with a red, white, and black leather Prada label on it, along with a black and white cherry blossom button up cotton shirt by Prada, with royal blue Prada pants, and black Prada shock absorb sole creeper shoes with some Prada aviator Sunglasses. Calm was wearing a soft smelling fragrance from Paul Sebastian that lingered inside the truck. The two enjoyed their intellectual conversation, as they continued to listen and reminisce to Aaliyah, while they discussed and disputed about the fashion industry. Calm felt that New York was the true foundation of the fashion industry, but Providence felt that Detroit's livelihood is the root of the fashion industry today. She claimed that Detroit's Fashion industry was full of stylish clothing that catered to the middle class, poor class and even rich class people. With clothing such as two-piece guess jeans suits, colourful guess jeans, short stretch tees, studded earrings, studded boots, studded belts, coach shoes and bags, Louis Vuitton shoes and bags.

During dinner Providence admired Calm's juicy lips as he ate his Greek salad slowly and carefully not to spill a drop of food or lettuce on his plate. While waiting for the main entrée, Providence unwrapped her gifts that she had purchased for Calm. She wanted him to know that he was a supportive person whom she appreciated and really cared for. Calm looked in her eyes as he softly inhaled the lavender tulips that she had purchased for him. The tulips were so soft, exotic, and expensive that he could not help but wonder about the price. Providence handed Calm the price tag along with the instruction pamphlet on how to care for the tulips. The two conversed as they shared a spinach quiche and ate Shrimp Pasta with lobster. During dessert the two giggled and shared some of their funniest and most intimate secrets. Providence laughed as she revealed her secret about her first kissing encounter with pickle juice.

Until this day Providence enjoys intimately kissing her boyfriends with pickle juice. The two giggled and laughed for minutes before Calm interrupted the laughter by waving his hand high and getting the waiters attention. He had wanted to try the pickle juice kiss for himself.

Waiter: "Hello."

Calm: "Hi yes, can I have a cup of pickles with pickle juice please."

When the waiter returned, Calm sipped the pickle juice from the monkey dish. He shared some of the pickle juice with Providence. He leaned towards Providence and softly kissed her on her lips. For 10 seconds the two just sat with their lips pressed against each other giggling as they enjoyed the pickle juice in their mouths. Suddenly Providence spotted a short brown skin girl with Indian hair rushing towards her, the girl leaped and swung on Providence. Providence dodged the punch; the girl swung again, almost landing a punch. Security raced to the scene and grabbed the assaulter who was attempting to assault Providence. Providence watched as the police carried her to the cop car. Calm was filling out a report as a witness. Providence felt violated and humiliated as she checked her face and body for scars and bruises. She opened her Chanel compact and checked her Brahmin crocodile skin suit. Thank God everything was still in place she thought as she covered her tracks. After the cop car pulled away Calm rushed over to Providence.

Providence: "Who was that, Calm? Your wife, your baby mother, your girlfriend?"

Calm apologised to her about his ex-girlfriend. Kema was her name, and she had followed the two around most of the afternoon. She had become deranged after a miscarriage and had developed serious jealousy issues. Kema had always allowed him to pay his rent and get money, but lately she had been in his way and was controlling his financial opportunities. Calm suggested an overnight stay at Rikers Island just to cool things down while he got to know Providence a little better. Calm knew that Providence felt discouraged about attending her first event as a DJ. He consoled her and reassured her that he would make it up to her with a nice foot massage on the way home, with a professional masseuse in the backseat. He hated the burden of a stalker especially while handling business, but he knew how much Kema wanted to bear his first child. Maybe they could try again in the future, but for now she needed a little time in Rikers Island to get her head together. Providence agreed to keep quiet about the situation without leaking the incident to the secret society as long as Calm's girlfriend Kema stayed away from her.

When the two arrived at the hall, the bouncers were waiting. One bouncer looked Calm in his eyes as he questioned him about his presence. Calm responded by stating that he and a new DJ were here from the Secret Society known as 31 Platinum Grills and they were here to host a main event and BYOB after party. Calm knew that bouncers needed to take precautions during these types of events that could sometime attract serial killers, mockers, copycats and other deranged people that bothered hairdressers and celebrities, so he took no real offense at the interrogation. Providence admired the chandeliers and decorations that were representations of gold paved roads around buildings, structures and city landscaping that resembled Italy and ancient Rome. The building was old, with antiques that smelled like fresh paints, waxed floor, and fresh carpets. The halls and carpets were filled with embroideries and royal designs with colours like gold, red and beige. The hall had been set up for the competition. Providence watched the crowd fill the room with stylish ponytails, up-do's, long hair weaves, freeze curls, and dreadlocks that were tucked twisted and dyed. The guests were wearing a variety of the most popular designer clothing from Louis Vuitton, Dolce and Gabbana, Chanel, Christian Dior, BCBG Maxazaria, Moschino and other designers. She watched as the host named Shaw set up the stage. Shaw was wearing a tailor-made matching Balmain dress that was similar to Providence's one-piece suit for the channel 7 interview. Her dress was short with a perfect fit. The bronze colours and crocodile skins accented her olive oiled skin and long legs. Shaw was carrying boxes of new microphones to the stage. She placed the microphones on the mic holders. Butterflies began to form as Providence watched Shaw announce the rules for the hair competition. Shaw announced the point scales for the winners which would be a 30-to-50-point scale. Some of the judging would be based on originality, firmness, control, and colours. The winners would win a grand total of 5,000 dollars; second and third place would win between 2,500 to 1,100 dollars. Fourth and Fifth place would win between 1,000 to 500 dollars and the losers would be given $200 gift certificates. All participants would receive gift certificates to Red Lobster and TJ Max, along with a free hair-do at Shaw's employer's Hair salon in New York City. Butterflies began to form as Providence waited for the event to begin. She squeezed Calm's hand and pleaded for him not to leave her side during the show. She opened the event with her original booty bouncing beats and cartoonist voices.

Verse 1
Blonde, Black, Blue hair weaves
No, you can't do it like me. No, you can't do it like me
Sew ins, Glue ins, Long Quick Weaves

No, you can't do it like me
No, you can't do it like me
Now, Clap, Clap, Clap
Now, Clap, Clap, Clap
Sew ins, Glue ins, Short Quick Weaves
No, you can't do it like me
No, you can't do it like me
Curly, wet, Brazilian Remy's
No, you can't do it like me
No, you can't do it like me
(Providence switches the music back and forth)
Studded boots, Studded pants
Now let me see you do that dance
Dance, Dance, Dance
Girls with big butts got razor cuts,
Slanted cuts, and layered cuts,
Cuts, Cuts, Cuts

The music banged as the audience went wild. The winner's name was Ray Daddy, a stylist who did a family of four. Ray Daddy removed all his stylist hair bags one by one. His first hair creation was titled 'St. Louis'. The hair creation was an enormous up do that had so many twist twirls and colours that it resembled the St. Louis monument. The next creation was called 'The Zoo Head Zebra' that was a high-top fade stair, stepped with different dyes and asymmetrical cuts. The last two models were wearing high ponytails with letterings that read 'Ray Daddy'. Other winners had hair creations called M&M's with M&M designs in their hair the models wore M&M jackets with stretch pants. Other winners designed short cuts with freeze curls, spiked cuts and designer bangs. Calm was pleased with Providence's performance. He offered her a recording contract and knew the perfect upcoming artist that she could work with. He wanted Providence in the studio within the next few weeks.

Once the event was over, the BYOB party began and Channel 7 News arrived. Shaw grabbed Providence for the interview.

News Anchor: "DJ Lady Lucina, what type of impact will tonight's performance have on your career in the future?"

Providence: "Well, honey, I have already been offered a recording contract and a fashion spread in a magazine which talks all about Lady Lucina. It can't get much better."

News Anchor: "Where did you get those fronts? They're darling."

Providence: "From a Secret Society of DJs known as 31 Platinum Grills."

News Anchor: "Oh, a secret society known as 31 Platinum Grills? Tell me more about this secret society."

Providence: "Well, it's an organisation of amateur DJs which began four years ago at the academy of DJs. The whole purpose of 31 Platinum Grills is to stick together as DJs and help one another in whatever ways we can."

(The news team talks amongst themselves for a few minutes)

News Team: "Well tonight my news team and I want to present a check for you and DJ Calm to share. Perhaps it will go to the secret society? Unfortunately, we could not interview DJ Calm tonight because he is busy rocking the after party, but as a token of our appreciation we are presenting you with a total of $20,000 in two checks, 10,000 for each."

(Providence begins to scream and jump up and down). She yells, "Thank You, Thank You, and Thank You." Providence begins to cry and scream at the same time on national television. She shows her appreciation by hugging the news team and smiling in the camera showing her fronts. Providence knew the rules about donations and charities. In the secret society there was a 10 percent rule. Any charity or donation that you receive you must report and give ten percent of your earnings. Providence smiled at the thought of pocketing nine grand during her first event. She was also happy to know that she and Calm would gain high recognition in the society by making a large contribution of $2,000 to the organisation.

Once the interview was over Providence mingled at the BYOB party, scoping out potential jobs.

The party was full of young people and old timers who performed dances like the electric slide on the dance floor. Providence obtained various job leads with a total of 27 signatures for the organisation to share at 31 Platinum.

Grills. The organisation was designed to assist one another by keeping all 31 members employed and busy by enforcing rules about sharing and reporting money and job leads to the organisation. After a long night the festivities had come to an end. During the ride home, Calm and Providence listened to loud music while drinking a bottle of $300 champagne. Providence felt relieved to know that after she strolled through avenue A and 1st avenue, and bar hopped all night, she would arrive home fully dressed from head to toe with a good respectable man, known as DJ Calm, who declined the offer to come in for coffee during the wee hours of the morning.

# Chapter 2

Calm sat at the table in disbelief, as he read the news headline that a girl had been brutally beaten and sexually assaulted in the backseat of a car by two police officers, on the way to Rikers Island for resisting arrest and spitting at an officer. Her name was Kema Anderson. Tears started to form as Calm thought about the brutality on top of the miscarriage that Kema recently had. He phoned Bouma, a jewellery storeowner and activist who often led rallies in the Garment District. Bouma had connections to the best attorneys in New York City and guaranteed Kema's release within a few days.

The next morning someone had bonded Kema out of jail. How did I get out on such a high bail? Kema wondered. She had been in jail for a week, which gave her plenty of time to think about the miscarriages and her assaults. She waved to a taxi driver but he did not stop. She dialled Calm's number. Calm answered the phone on the third ring.

Calm: "Hello?"

Kema: "I need some money, Western Union, to get off of Rikers Island, please." (Calm could hear Kema crying)

Calm: "It should be there in ten minutes. Kema; listen, I have been thinking maybe we should meet up. You catch a cab to the Waldorf Astoria. Let's sleep and relax and make things right. I want to vacation with you for a week."

Kema was short and dark-skinned with a medium build and long Indian hair. Her dark smooth skin and Indian hair always turned him on and gave him an instant erection. Calm was always ready and willing to have intercourse with her, but lately, she had often been interfering with his money. He wanted to ease her mind about the new involvements with girls and the investments. He promised to ease her mind tonight and start fresh. Calm loved Kema's Indian hair and her brown skin. Her sex appeal drove him wild. He had purchased her a hot pink v cut lace body suit, lingerie from Victoria's secret. He wanted to make love to her in the shower and requested that she purchase motion shampoo so he could gently wash her hair.

Kema caught a taxi to the Waldorf Astoria in New York City. Several thoughts ran through her mind as she searched for answers; why, how could Calm press charges against me for acting out?

Kema considered the incident at the restaurant: That lady deserved to be swung on for kissing my man! Kema had spent years moulding Calm, setting up shows for him and making moves for him. How could some hussy still steal her man, she thought? Kema knew if she could convince Calm to give her one more chance that she would produce a baby boy or girl for him. She had visited the fertility clinic, and they had helped her to plan for a baby. She reminisced about Calm and their lovemaking while trying for a baby. He often made her moan so loud till it seemed her head spun and she fell unconsciously asleep. One time she and Calm had made love all night, and the sex was so overwhelming that she had passed out and slept most of the next day. How could he press charges on her, she thought? Calm had promised he would make it up to her tonight with down comforter spreads that were nice, warm, and fluffy, for the two to cuddle in. When she arrived he was all ready for lovemaking, and he expected Kema to be hot and ready after she showered. Providence was a special and talented new DJ that he wanted, but Kema was reality for him. Calm put his phone on vibrate after he phoned Providence to schedule a meeting for next week on avenue A. When Kema arrived Calm noticed bruises on her. The police had beaten her up for resisting arrest. She could barely walk after being slammed on her back. Calm grabbed her gently and kissed her on her forehead. She cried endlessly. She had felt a violent thrust in between her legs while the guards checked her for weapons. Thank god he had dropped the charges. She promised him she would never interfere with any of his female partners or moneymaking opportunities. She told Calm an inmate had attempted to rape her and pimp her and she never wanted to go back to Rikers Island ever. Kema and Calm checked into the Waldorf Astoria building. The two enjoyed the view of the city after they bathed and put on matching robes.

Calm placed hot towels on Kema's body all night. He massaged her body until she fell sound asleep. He rubbed his fingers through her hair when she awoke they would make love endlessly, he thought.

The Oaths and Rules of 31 Platinum Grills Secret Society
Motto: Slow money is always good money.

All problems within the organisation must stay within the organisation and are always to be resolved within the organisation.

Rule #1 No Selling Drugs
Rule # 2 No Drug Dealers allowed
Rule # 3 No dope fiends allowed
Motto#2 Fast money is bad money.

What happens if you get caught disobeying the rules? You face fines and trial with the secret society and 31 Platinum Grills.

Initiation into 31 Platinum Grills.

31 Platinum Grills initiations consist of skilled dentistry practices and artistic creations which take place in a small laboratory for a two-week period. During this timeframe, it's each member's task to perfectly design 31 gold and platinum mouthpiece fronts by taking mouth impressions of the 31 members, including the professor and excluding yourself, which keeps it at 31 members. The members are given 14-carat chip pieces to work with, that are donated from a jewellery store with an owner named Bouma, in the Garment District.

New Problem this week is that a long-term member named Raul, who has been with the secret society for three years, is suspected of violating the organisation after DJ Calm set up a secret sting with.

Raul, who has been serving cocaine to some of his clients after his DJ performances. Calm just recently found out that Raul is one of the biggest Cuban dealers in Spanish Harlem and owns a restaurant on the Upper East Side. He is said to be worth over a million dollars and acquired all this money through the secret society job leads and placements.

Raul worked the night shift as the neighbourhood coke dealer. He cruised through the neighbourhoods late nights, low key in a white T-shirt and chef pants. Raul was tired of the same old routes with clients and murder mommies that he had met during the DJ performances. He made his rounds with the girls in the passenger seats who purchased coke from him. He switched cars at least three times a night. He was tired of the same old mommies and women who powder their noses and made freaky gestures while high. Although he had opportunities to have sex with them, he passed up the opportunities because he knew it was the effects from good coke that made them freaky. At the end of the night, when he was done making his rounds and switching cars, he would pretend to be tired instead of engaging in any sexual offers. Raul was a 26-year-old brown skin Cuban virgin, who was six feet tall. His body appeared to be full of testosterone. His body was so toned and built you could see the bulge from his calf muscles through his pants and his bicep muscles through his T-shirts. Raul was a handsome Cuban who had gigantic moles on his face. He had become a dealer on the nightshift 3 years ago. Although he engaged in illegal activity on New York City streets, his beliefs about sex before marriage were solid to him and the family who vowed to select the perfect wife for Mr. Raul Santos. Nobody knew the secret about his virginity, but at this point Raul had felt that he had found the perfect girl, named Providence, who he wanted to pursue as his wife and give all of his love to. Raul always respected women, but then women never gave him any respect. Women often went bananas over his coke rubbing and touching him begging him for mercy and blowjobs, but he never budged. He knew that next to Puerto Rico, he had the best coke. Raul could look at breasts and butts and feel as though they were natural objects and features that women were born with. He always felt this way, ever since he was a little boy. He felt that a woman did not deserve to be touched or stared at unwillingly. His father always said he was an Arabian in a Cuban's body. Raul was a millionaire now who accumulated most of his clients from DJ parties sanctioned by the secret society. Years later, after he had accumulated over a million dollars, he had opened a small restaurant on the Upper East Side. Raul knew the rules about selling drugs and the possibilities of being dismissed from 31 Platinum Grills, but he thought the chance was impossible of being caught until one day he sold to an undercover member by the name of DJ Calm, the founder of the Secret Society.

Raul was relaxing in Spanish Harlem on a hot sunny day. He was playing on the lawn with some of the other kids on the block. His cooler on the lawn was filled with free water and soda for the kids to have. Raul had passed out over 30 drinks in less than 5 minutes. News travelled fast in Spanish Harlem about free items, he thought. After the kids finished drinking and playing football. Raul sat on the porch in a lawn chair until sundown before making his runs. He started the night off good with a $2,000 coke sale on 8th street in New York City. Raul pulled up to the curb to wait for the purchaser. Suddenly DJ Calm and a secret society member approached the car. Calm presented Raul with summons to trial papers, to hear his testimonies. The date was stamped a week from today which gave him a week to prepare his defence. Raul was given the choice to resign or pay a $6,000 fine and stand trial. With all the money he had, he chose to stand trial. During trial Raul pleaded with the trial members. In his testimony he revealed that he was a 26-year virgin with the responsibility of supporting his large family from Cuba, Mexico, and Puerto Rico, who all lived together in Spanish Harlem. After weeks of deliberations and no job placements Raul had won the trial and the jury members had voted him back into the society, because of his efforts to remain a virgin until marriage. Deep down inside Raul knew that the Secret Society was scared to dismiss him. They feared retaliation from one of his family members who could be coming from all parts of the world. But the only one that they truly had to worry about was Rosa, who Raul had taken care of since she was in junior high. She was the hit maker and could find out anything that Raul needed to know.

# Chapter 3

Bouma, a jewellery storeowner and activist from the Garment District, organised a rally for women against Police Brutality and sexual assaults. The rally was organised for Calm whose girlfriend had been brutally attacked and sexually assaulted, after resisting arrest. Bouma wanted to help women who had experienced sexual assaults on subways, or city streets late at night. He also wanted to speak out against police brutality, and violence against women. Bouma had booked several motivational speakers, including an Arabian woman who had been dismembered and brutally beaten by the police in Afghanistan, a woman from London would be speaking who had been sexually assaulted and raped during a big party event, and a woman from India who had been brutally gang raped. The rallies offered services for women who had these types of experiences all around the world. Counsellors and therapists helped Bouma place pamphlets on the tables with their work addresses or 'on site' locations. The rally would be filled with fun and entertainment today. Bouma set up the tents as the heat burned his back. Bouma was a short dark skinned British jewellery storeowner who had come to the Garment District from London several years ago. He became an activist for workers' rights and violence against women by spreading his testimonies about the suffering and poverty he endured with a family of eleven. Bouma placed the HIV awareness pamphlets with condom sets on the tables. He noticed that Kema and Calm had arrived. Kema's arm was still bruised from her handcuffs and assaults. Bouma felt her pain and hoped that this rally would reach the media and help her upcoming trial and civil suit. The rally went on for hours, as you heard testimonies and cries throughout the yard. The event was full of hotdogs, hamburgers, steaks, potato salad, drinks and fun games. During the event Calm and Kema cried onstage with the other motivational speakers. Women reached out and spoke up about their situations regarding domestic violence. The rally had ended during the evening. Bouma and Calm counted the proceeds and charity money that was donated for Kema's trial. Kema was happy to know that she would be financially stable during her trial. She was also happy to know that she had a support system. Calm was thankful to know that Bouma was by her side. He ended the night with a smile and a partial charity check for his friend Bouma in the amount of $500 dollars for his services.

Providence waved to the taxi driver on Broadway and Myrtle. She was meeting the Secret Society of 31 Platinum Grills at BBQ's, a famous restaurant near Jay Street in downtown Brooklyn. The restaurant was famous for its barbecue entrées and other inexpensive entrées. BBQ's was a popular lounging spot for African Americans from all over the world. Calm had booked a group reservation for the organisation to celebrate and accept Providence's contribution to the Secret Society, after her outstanding first performance during the International hair show. He wanted to recognise the amateur DJ by presenting her with a reward and a plaque from 31 Platinum Grills. Providence was greeted with applauses by 31 Platinum Grills when she entered the restaurant. She took a seat nervously as she reached into her manila envelope and pulled out the 2,000-dollar check that she and Calm had contributed from their charity checks from channel 7. Unfortunately, Calm was unable to attend. He had replaced his appearance with the treasurer and one of the original organisers, named Kevin, who was there to present Providence with an overachiever's award. As an honour, Kevin granted Providence the right to pick and choose her next four job placements from a list. Providence smiled at the waiter as he placed her special vodka drink on the table. The restaurant was loud and noisy and, after a few drinks, Providence found herself half-screaming during conservations. She noticed Raul eyeing her during dinner. The society had ordered a total of 100 wings, full of different flavours. Raul was amazed at Providence's accomplishments. He had been with the Secret Society for 3 years and had never made more than 800 dollars in a night. Just recently he had been ordered to pay a $6,000 fine for violating the organisation. He felt that it was amazing that Providence was able to contribute more than most of the DJs had made in a night. Raul admired Providence's stunning personality, her freshly permed hair and white Versace shades, along with her white and gold V-neck maxi dress that flowed almost to the bottom of her white leather wedges with wood grain. Raul wanted the opportunity to get to know her, so he figured he should offer to take her shopping at Barneys for her upcoming photo shoot and fashion spread with Shaw and NYC Hair Magazine. He offered to cover the expenses for the photo shoot as long as she agreed to have dinner with him at his own restaurant on the upper East-side. Providence could not believe that Raul was a virgin, that he had never had a sexual encounter. She could not help but notice, desire and recognise Raul for his wealth. She desperately needed to be Mrs. Santos for a day, flooded in money, with a faithful man. Luckily, Raul had offered to take her shopping at Barneys for her upcoming photo shoot with Shaw in NYC Hair magazine. He felt that it was the least he could do with all his illegal money. The two had set a date for dinner at his upscale restaurant on the upper East-side and shopping at Barney's with a 3,000 dollars limit. After the two finished conversing, Providence had announced that she was dropping all of the charges against Kema, Calm's girlfriend, who had subsequently been brutally beaten after resisting arrest. Bouma's rally about violence against women and police brutality had touched Providence and changed her decision about pressing charges. Providence glanced back over at Raul, as she admired Raul's testosterone-toned body and his beauty moles on his face. Deep down inside she wanted to find his vulnerability, so she could find her way into his life. From there, she would live the life of a millionaire. Raul smiled at Providence. He checked the number on his phone and read the text message from Rosa that the evening's take was good. Finally it was his last shipment; he and Rosa were out the drug game for good.

Providence rushed home to Broadway and Bushwick to change her clothes. She had lived on Broadway in Brooklyn all her life, but had dreams of living in a mansion with Mr Santos. For once, she did not have to worry about her sex appeal, as her husband to be was still a virgin and knew nothing about sex. She flat ironed her hair and slipped on a long V-neck floral maxi dress. She accessorised her dress with matching Chanel shoes and earrings. She decided to be ghetto and catch the train instead of spending the taxi money that Raul had given her to meet him on the Upper East Side. When Providence arrived, Raul was sitting with a restaurant manager from a nearby restaurant, conversing about business in the area. Raul was wearing a nice Prada coat, which looked like a velour material. He had prepared for Providence a wonderful meal with sautéed butter-peeled crab legs, well-seasoned fish, along with hand-picked string beans with white peanuts and white wine. Raul gave her a sexy grin, showing the side of his teeth, as he and Providence enjoyed their meals and talked over their candlelight dinner. The two conversed for hours while Providence cried, smearing her eye liner. She spilled her feelings to Raul and confessed that she had fallen for DJ Calm, who was madly in love with another woman that had attacked her at the restaurant. Now that she realised how serious their love was, she had lost the feelings for Calm and was now ready to record the album as only business partners. The two conversed for hours.

Raul was from Spanish Harlem and had lived there all of his life, with his extended family, grandparents and parents. Raul decided to prepare the meal in the early afternoon, so the two could shop at Barneys during the evening. On the way to Barney's, Providence quickly changed her mind as she thought they had such a casual selection that it would not be vibrant enough in her photo shoot. Although she knew it was slightly ghetto, she wanted more vibrant neon and pastel colours for her shoot next week. Before she knew it, she was on her way to Miami to visit one of the most vibrant stores entitled 'We Love Colours' on the North West side in Miami. During the visit, Providence was assisted in every which way with her photo shoot. The sales associates had suggested neon and zigzag thigh high socks, splash coloured leotards and unitards, splash coloured matte leggings, fish net leggings, and other metallic and micro fibre items. The two had managed to shop the very next day and make it home during the same night. When the two arrived home, Providence offered Raul a light compensation with a few sex tricks that she had learned to do with her hands. She managed to be the first to touch and put Raul on cloud nine without removing one piece of clothing from her body.

Providence was amazed at her fashion spread with the first founder of 31 Platinum Grills. The spread had been placed on the cover of NYC Hair Magazine. The cover read: How DJ Calm found DJ Lady Lucina. Inside the cover it read: The first founder, DJ Calm, of the secret society named 31 Platinum Grills, has discovered and produced an upcoming artist and DJ who's famous for her booty bouncing, rump shaking beats with the impressionist voices of cartoonist vocalist. Look out for the ladies upcoming album that's filled with Detroit's remixed native music and rocking booty bouncing beats.

The fashion spread was unbelievable. Providence's shoot was filled with vibrant neon colours and her Mohawk was streaked with colourful tracks. Her eyes looked alive and her lips looked thick and smooth. Calm had officially put her on in the music industry and now there was no turning back.

Providence met Calm at his studio on Avenue A in New York City to finish her upcoming album duo with a new artist that he had discovered. The two needed to discuss and agree on the location of the album release party. Calm had recently remodelled the studio and had added a small room to the building. When Providence opened the door to the small room where she thought Calm would be she noticed two males sitting on the couch covering their private parts with towels and a skinny pregnant brown skin girl with milky big breast that hung from her spaghetti strap biker dress. The girl appeared to be four or five months pregnant. She looked at Providence and responded by saying that she needed to pay rent and would be reserving this spot for the night taking all artist who were paying well that were in need of blow jobs. Providence shut the door as she made her way into the big studio; she reminded herself why she had chosen her occupation in the first place. Tears formed as she walked into the large studio room. Calm noticed Providence crying, he reassured her that the pregnant woman was too money hungry and was caught up in a rich lifestyle. Calm knew her baby daddy personally and knew that he had reasonable wages but his baby mother was obsessed with expensive hairdos, designer clothing and upscale parties and was willing to do whatever it took to cop Christian Dior even with a baby in her stomach. After hours of deliberation Calm and Providence had agreed that the perfect location for the album release party would be in Washington, D.C.

Providence and Calm rehearsed their new song:

I make it special like a BCBG booming feature
Spotlight like a Mexicano Senorita
Addicted to Prada scents Versace fumes
Mobster like a Cole Haan Trench
Fortunato Jewels
I wanna vanish out of town
They call it therapy

I wanna vanish out of town
Boy won't you marry me
Boy won't you wife me
Don't act so scheisty
Choosy lover on my level
Won't you marry me?
Choosy lover on my level
Don't act so scary
I wanna vanish out of town
Boy won't you marry me
Choosy lover on my level
Don't act so scary
I make it special
So very special
I make it fly
So very fly.

Providence and Calm finished the album; He phoned the D.C nightclub for reservations. He was sure that Providence would make it a night that they and all of D.C would never forget.

# Chapter 4

Rosa hated the idea of catching a train to another neighbourhood to see her new boyfriend. Brooklyn was a lot different from Spanish Harlem, she thought, as she rushed to the three train to get to Borough hall near downtown Brooklyn and Jay Street on an early Sunday morning. She wanted it to be a surprise for Orlando, her new African American boyfriend at his dollar store in downtown Brooklyn. She planned to spend the whole day with him on Jay Street, working all day. Orlando had been her new secret love interest that she had been creeping around with for the last few months. Although she knew it was wrong, she promised Raul a stash spot and had found that Orlando's dollar store was a perfect secret hiding place. Rosa had used her charm to ease her way into Orlando's life and had finally found the opportunity to go through with her plans. Orlando was preparing for inventory. He had a good feeling that his percentage loss and store shrink was going to be low during inventory, since he had watched for thieves' every day. He counted the shampoos and hair gels on the shelf in the dollar store. He scanned the items with a scanner that his inventory group had given him. It was Sunday morning and the store would be opening in the next three hours, after his inventory team had left at 11:00 a.m. He thought about Rosa as he scanned the items on the shelf. He loved her silky skin, dark brown eyes and her wavy hair. Orlando admired Rosa's softness and gentleness but wanted to remain close friends with her because of his work ethic and location in downtown Brooklyn. The location was too upbeat to have a steady girlfriend and besides he was a dollar storeowner, who worked like an Arabian storeowner. Orlando worked a 13-hour workday and a six-day workweek and was looking for an employee to relieve him. Soon he would be hiring Rosa to work with him, if he found her trustworthy. His life revolved around the store and he hadn't had sex in years. In the last relationship that he was in, years ago, he often used Viagra for his sexual activity, because of his obsessive work ethic. Orlando knew Rosa would be disappointed by this, so he wanted to find her a good husband and promised to do so if it was the last thing that he'd do. Rosa arrived at the dollar store wearing a hot pink and Gray DKNY, shiny spandex, and tennis shoes with thick soles and a symbol that read DKNY. She was wearing a fresh white DKNY top with white DKNY ankle socks to match. She was ready to work and had her hair secured in a bun. She carried a picnic basket full of fruits and vegetables with papaya and mango juice, along with some Cuban steak sandwiches. Although she needed a vulnerable person to stash Raul's final shipment of drugs, she had fallen for Orlando and couldn't wait to see him. When the two hugged, she caught chills as she inhaled his cologne and squeezed his back. Orlando felt the intensity from Rosa's hug. He knew that she was a genuine person who would make a good wife someday. He kissed her softly on her cheek and sighed. Once the inventory was completed he opened up the store doors and prepared for the busy day. Orlando enjoyed the cool breeze that drifted through the door as he trained Rosa on the register. He showed her how to watch for thieves in the store isles by using the secret monitor that he placed below the register. The secret cameras had four monitor screens that showed clear views of the customers inside and outside. Orlando explained to Rosa the policy about business and pleasure. He wanted her to know that this was not the place to have a jealous heart, that feelings should be stabilised as he knew tons of African American men and women in the downtown neighbourhood. He explained to Rosa how to disregard invitations to parties and dinners and how to keep the relationship at a minimal with customers. He last explained to her the term known as bribery which meant doing something in exchange for something else. Never accept money for storage, especially for drugs, like cocaine or heroin. Rosa knew bribes were unacceptable, but her whole reason for taking the job in the city was to store Raul's drugs in Orlando's basement for a couple of months while the two waited to transport their last shipment. Rosa would figure out a way to manipulate him into believing in her and then, on Orlando's off day, she would transport the drugs and money. She just needed her first day alone to find a storage spot in between the old wood of the basement. During the week, Rosa and one of Orlando's regular customers began disputing in the store isles after Rosa asked her if she needed help looking for something. The African American girl became offended and replied with a racist remark that Columbians were taking over. Before Orlando knew it, fists began to fly from the regular customer and suddenly the two were on the floor pulling hair and disputing. Orlando let the two girls fight without calling the police. He knew that if Rosa was going to begin to relieve him with a five-day workweek schedule that she would have to know how to defend herself. When the fight was over the customer responded to Orlando by saying that he was a racist and wouldn't hire someone from his own race to work in the store. She yelled down Jay Street that Orlando was a racist and didn't trust his own kind to work for him. Rosa was being paid $11 an hour to run the store. Even though she liked the pay and Orlando, her real reason for working was to find a stash spot for Orlando's drugs and money. She couldn't wait to transport the drugs on Sunday, she thought, as she watched the monitor on Jay Street in case the girl came back. Rosa knew it was wrong, but the time had come for her to end the relationship with Orlando. After a few months had passed, Orlando opened up the store and found a thank you note on the counter from Rosa, stating that she and her family had decided to open up their own dollar store in Spanish Harlem. She apologised for the abrupt notice of termination, but promised that as soon as things got settled she would come to see him again.

Kema had her suspicions about Providence and Calm's event in D.C. For some reason, Kema envisioned the two sexing after an event in the hotel room. Although she had heard that Calm reserved two rooms, she couldn't help but worry that Providence would take her man. Kema voiced her opinion to Raul about Calm and Providence. He responded by saying that if it worried her, that he would tag along to the event as long as she promised not to be too controlling. Raul never knew how charming Kema was, to his surprise, the two had a several things in common. The more the two conversed the more he began to admire her. Kema confided in Raul about her and Calm's relationship. She cried on his shoulders about her suffering from an incident that had recently occurred between her, Calm and Providence. Kema had suffered from major depression after her attempted assault, which resulted in weeks of incarceration on Rikers Island. During that time Kema had suffered from a miscarriage and police brutality, which resulted from her resisting arrest, because of her boyfriend's kissing incident with his new client. Kema had her suspicions about Providence and Calm's album release party. She wanted to make sure that Calm knew she meant business about their relationship. As weeks passed, Raul and Kema held secret conversations over the telephone late at night while their lovers were asleep. The two conversed for many hours about marriage, children, family, education, fashion, and beauty. As weeks had grown, Kema and Raul discovered that they had more in common than they thought and they began hanging out as street buddies. As more time passed, Raul decided to secretly invite Kema to a boxing match in Puerto Rico, as a token of friendship. He wanted to have a lady on his arm, and since Providence and Calm were busy making the album, they would never notice Raul's and Kema's disappearance. Kema rushed to Queens's airport where she was meeting Raul for the flight to Puerto Rico. Kema was wearing a high low chiffon dress, the top of the dress was shaped like an ivy lace strapless boos Tieu top with a high low chiffon skirt attached. Kema was wearing some ivy and beige lace wedges with peanut butter leather soles. Raul was wearing a soft coral Ralph Lauren Polo shirt with some beige polo shorts and soft brown leather crotchet sandals. Raul and Kema rushed to board the flight. The two stepped on the flight happily, as they searched for their seats. Suddenly, Kema noticed a white male walking past her. He stared at her, as he walked past her, and whispered to her softly in her ear, "You're dead, Kema! You're dead before trial, and you deserved to be beat to death! Make your last wish, Kema, because you only have 20 seconds to live before I blow this plane up." Kema watched the white male run off the plane. She reached franticly for her phone, but it was too late. Within seconds, the plane had exploded and burst into flames, killing both Kema and Raul instantly.

Calm and Providence turned up the radio in the studio to hear the announcement that Calm the first founder of the Secret Society known as 31 Platinum Grills' girlfriend Kema had been killed in a plane crash along with DJ Lady Lucina's soon to be husband/fiancé, named Raul. The two had been killed when an airplane was exploded with a bomb. Foul play is suspected and the bombing could be police related, due to an upcoming trial and a pending lawsuit that Kema had filed. It was said that Kema and Raul were secretly heading to Puerto Rico to attend a boxing match, possibly smuggling large amounts of money. Calm and Providence rushed to JFK airport in the nearest taxi. Neither one was well enough to drive.

# Chapter 5

Rosa searched through the old wooden floors for Raul's shipment. Although she knew it was selfish, she had plans to leave Orlando tonight and start her new life as a storeowner in Spanish Harlem. Rosa wrote her thank you letter and placed it on the counter along with the keys to the store. She felt good to know that she had made it out the game and out of illegal activity. She read the letter once more, making sure her message was clear about her reason for quitting her job. The message was a thank you note thanking him for trusting her and allowing her to work in his dollar store. Also, she wanted to let him know that she appreciated his efforts in training her to properly run a dollar store of her own in Spanish Harlem. She promised to visit him again as soon as her new dollar store in Spanish Harlem showed some financial gains. Rosa grabbed the shipment and headed for JFK in her parents Mercedes Truck. She arrived at the airport with Raul's packages. Raul had instructed her to take the package to gate number eight at approximately 8:30pm. His uncle would be working the baggage check. Raul instructed Rosa to check the nametag for a guy name Jose. She waited until approximately 8:30pm before she approached the gate wearing an urban neon T-shirt that Raul had instructed her to wear in order to be properly identified by his uncle. She grabbed her duffle bag and rushed down towards Jose's gate before his departure. She placed the duffle bag onto the converter belt and walked through the metal detector. Jose smiled at her as he handed her another duffle bag with half a million dollars in it. She rushed towards Raul's gate, where she found him with a short brown-skinned girl with Indian hair waiting to board a private plane. Raul smiled with relief as he picked up the abandoned duffle bag that she left on a chair. Rosa watched the two board the plane. As soon as the two were out of sight she rushed towards the nearest exit to the JFK airport and jumped into her parents Mercedes truck. She turned her ignition and suddenly she heard a loud explosion. Raul's plane was exploding into pieces right before her eyes. Rosa felt frantic as she realised Raul was gone, along with a half a million dollars. She raced to the JFK exit where security had blocked off all entrances and exits. Sounds of sirens from police cars and fire trucks filled her ears. Rosa got out and stood in the parking lot in disbelief. Thoughts ran through her mind about how would she survive without him? Just recently he had purchased a dollar store in her name and had given her $20,000 in start-up money and petty cash. All the merchandise had come with the store and it was up to Rosa to maintain it. She got back in the vehicle and exited the parking lot before the police could secure it. She drove a half a mile away before she phoned her parents and gave them the bad news that Raul had just died in an airplane explosion at JFK airport in Queens New York.

"Turn up the radio louder," Calm shouted as he rushed the taxi driver. Providence and Calm both placed their phones on vibrate, as they watched them ring off the hook from calling reporters who wanted to be the first to comment about their significant others' deaths. The taxi driver sped through side streets, rushing to JFK airport. He listened to the host from the radio program urging people to buy candles on their way to JFK to support the victims. Calm's stomach sank as he answered the phone and requested that the radio station play Aaliyah Rock the boat on the radio so he and Providence could feel consoled about what they were about to encounter. The two sat in the backseat crying to Aaliyah. Calm ran into 7 Eleven demanding candles. The store clerk could see that he was disturbed as he ordered Calm not to worry he would get as many as he needed off the shelf and from the back. When Providence and Calm arrived near the airport, candles could be spotted from a mile away like lampshades in a river. The sound of mourning families, friends and significant others could be heard from afar. Calm had never known how bad family members felt during September 911, when horrible terrorist attacks had occurred, but to both him and Providence, 911 had occurred all over again. For hours they awaited the news about their respective loved ones.

Families were sleeping in ditches in cars and vans waiting for the news that their loved ones and significant others were or were not on the flight to Puerto Rico. Suddenly the announcement had come. It stated that Kema Anderson and Raul Santos were on the flight and were assumed killed. Providence cried frantically as she thought about her upcoming wedding and wedding invitations that she had just mailed out a week ago. All that was gone now, and although she tried to avoid the situation, somehow Providence and Calm had ended up back together again, back at square one. Weeks later, some news about flight 437 to Puerto Rico was spreading. The flight had exploded from a bomb that was placed underneath a passenger seat. Possible police involvement to dodge an upcoming trial had been ruled out, and there was possible foul play at hand. The planes explosion was blamed on a terrorist attack. But although the police were ruled out as suspects, Calm knew deep down the police had killed Kema and Raul to prevent her lawsuit.

Bouma organised the rally with activists against police brutality and violence against women. Speakers and family members arrived to secretly mourn the deaths of their loved ones aboard flight 437. The crowd felt that it would be best to mourn in secret, since rumours had spread in the media that the police had possibly committed the terrorist act and it had been covered up by the government. It had been weeks since the incident, and everyone was ready to pour out their feelings about the issue and the possibility about the police getting rid of people. The rally had turned into an informative meeting, filled with government secrets. People who felt upset and wanted to share things about their feelings towards the police screamed and shouted out their conspiracy theories. Bouma encouraged everyone to release their inner feelings before the end of the night, no matter how humiliated they felt. The rally went on until the wee hours of the evening. Marijuana smoke filled the room, for some of the victims loved ones could not handle the emotion without some comfort. At the end of the night Providence sat there in tears wearing her new wedding dress that she had showcased and testified about. Calm and Bouma were there to console her about the tragic loss of her ex-fiancé. During the rally, the police had secretly broke into Calm's apartment and tampered with his foods and beverages, adding memory loss substances and other food poisonings to prevent him from pursuing the case about Kema's police brutality any further. The police had decided that periodic food tampering would be the best solution to Calm's curiosity. That way, there would be no more accidents.

# Chapter 6

Calm could feel that he had been poisoned but the psychiatric facility felt that he had only become too paranoid after he attempted to have a discussion with the police on several occasions about Kema's murder. The psychiatric facility decided to keep him for a year after his repeated offenses and attacks on the police became all too familiar. His clothing had changed from high priced clean clothing to dingy, smelly old materials. Calm had begun to get high and spent most of his time hanging out in Marcy projects, rolling Vega blunts. The once producer that Providence had known and received her motivation from had turned into a low-life with no direction. Providence knew the brown-skinned girl with Indian hair was his life. She had put him on and had whipped it on him from sun down to sun up on several occasions. Providence had decided to give Calm a surprise visit at his apartment in Brooklyn. When Calm answered the door in his boxer shorts, the smell of gym socks and marijuana lingered from his apartment. He looked Providence in her eyes and suddenly smacked her. He accused her of having his girlfriend killed in order to get close to him. Calm accused her of setting him up and slipping him mickeys every day. Providence stared at Calm hurt and ashamed of what had just happened. She stared at him and pleaded for her time to speak. She held him and consoled him as she whispered to him softly in his ears that she would always be here for him, not because she was the one who wanted him, but because she was the one who was a true friend through thick and thin. She pleaded with him to let her into his heart and mind as she soothed him and gave him a peppermint bath just like Kema had done, just like he requested, but he would not budge and the more and more violent he became the more she had no choice but to call the psychiatric unit and have him admitted, where they kept him for a year.

New Rules and Motto's

All men rule!

All girls are hoes!

Men make money!

Hoes don't!

After Calm's breakdown, his accountant Kevin resigned. The organisation known as The Secret Society of 31 Platinum Grills was left in shambles and some twins had decided to take upon themselves to run the organisation for the year that Calm was gone. The twins had been part of the organisation for three years and had felt that they could run the organisation better than anyone, now that Calm was gone. The proper procedures and voting process as well as elections had become totally obsolete as the twins bullied their way into power, making women powerless creatures. The twins' first rule was that all men ruled and all women were hoes and worthless creatures who needed to be at home where they belonged; making babies and cooking dinner or pimped in the small studio room, inside of Calm's studio. The twins were quite short, brown skinned, muscular, and ruthless 24-year-olds from Cleveland, Ohio, who came to New York to live with their father after a drive by shooting had killed their mother. Their names were Ace and Bishop. Ace and Bishop had decided to turn the girl members of the Secret Society into sex slaves while they set up all the male members with job leads. They had always wanted to present the possibility to Calm but were too scared of trials, members, and prosecutions. Providence received a text message from Ace. She rushed to Calm's studio after she had received the message stating that he had wanted to work on her new album. She hurried into the studio happily as she opened the small room to see if the same pregnant girl was occupying the room for blowjobs. To her surprise Ace and Bishop were waiting there with guns and johns who were looking to have sex with nice looking girls. When she arrived Ace had greeted her with a smile as he placed the gun near Providence's head and ordered her to take off her clothes and turn a trick for 200 hundred dollars in the room with magnum condoms. For weeks Providence was forced to turn tricks doing at least three or four johns a day in the studio room. Her life and career had vanished before her eyes and she felt worthless and lifeless. How could she go from being an upcoming artist with a new album to a sex slave in the same small studio? This was the situation that she vowed to never be in; the same thoughts that motivated her to finish her album not long ago. She had cried on calm's shoulder over the pregnant girl who was willing to be a sex worker and now she had become that person, only it was not under 'free will' but force. How could Calm let this happen, leaving her high and dry, accusing her of things that she had not really done? Six months had passed and Providence had lost her figure. She had slept days, on the worn-out mattress, at a time. One day Ace surprised her with a gift. It was a new big screen T.V. He promised that Providence could watch it on her free time when it was not being used to make sex tapes and entertain johns with porno's. Ace spent his days taping Providence, creating sex tapes for the sex industry. Deep down inside Providence knew her life and career had ended. Providence felt that the twins were some type of omen that prophesised the devil's return. She felt as though this was the future for young girls. Young men were turning into monsters, forcing women and girls into sex slavery. How could the twins take her life from her at the drop of a dime? How could they not take her to trial and hear her testimonies before sentencing her to life as a sex slave and a prostitute. Providence had only had sex with about 50 men all her life and she was 26 years old. Ace and Bishop had forced her to have sex with more people in a month than she had sex with in her entire life since she was 15. One morning Providence awoke to the sounds of hip-hop music. She heard laughter and sounds as she lay on the worn-out mattress. She had done several tricks in an eight-hour time span and was completely parched, starved and tired. She could hear the sound of a cart being rolled out of the big studio and down the hall. Suddenly she heard footprints in front of the door she hoped that it was not another John as her body could not take anymore. Bishop knocked at the door, suddenly he burst through the room with a stainless-steel plate and a small birthday cake that read Happy 27th Birthday Providence. Providence smiled as she remembered that today was her birthday. The twins presented her with a gourmet lunch, white wine, cake and ice cream, shopping, an overnight stay at a shabby hotel in New Jersey, and a two-minute phone call to her mom. Providence phoned her mum excitedly, when she picked up, she relieved her with three words; "I'm alive mom," and then nine more words, "I Love you and I will be home soon." Ace hung up the phone as he ordered Providence to grab her things for her first time outdoors in a year, tonight she could do whatever her heart desired as long as the twins were nearby watching her every move.

Bouma was happy to hear back from the psychiatric facility, granting him a visitation to visit Calm. He hurried to the NYC Psych facility where Calm had been for the last two years. He grabbed his badge and checked his items. Bouma wanted to ease his mind about questions regarding the police involvement with Kema's death. Apparently there had been some Ku Klux Klan member, a follower who terrorised her about pressing charges against white police officers. The Ku Klux Klan member felt that white police officers should never have to stand trial from a black girl, so he decided to blow the plane to pieces after following Kema's story closely. Apparently the Ku Klux Klan member had been watching her for months and had followed her to the airport where he placed a bomb aboard the plane. Kema's and Raul's family had been compensated with and given over a million dollars each to ease the pain and suffering that the family had endured. It had been two years since Bouma had last seen Calm, since he had been hospitalised. He hoped deep down inside that Calm was ready to come home as he had a quarter million waiting for him when he got well. Apparently the police had been slipping Calm memory loss substances all these years because he was accusing the officers of placing bombs on airplanes to prevent the case from going to trial. Today Calm would find out it was some hate group that was behind his girlfriend's death and the police indeed had nothing to do with it. Bouma was shocked to see Calm's appearance. His skin appeared white and chalky his hair was beaded and nappy and his body was skinny and curved. His eyes appeared bugged instead of low and sleepy the way they had always appeared. Calm hugged Bouma tightly while he cried on his shoulder, he slipped a napkin full of food into his pocket while he whispered in Bouma's ear, "They're poisoning me man, I can't think man, I'm turning white in here, and pale, I can't even zip my pants or tie my shoes anymore, they got me dun, have that tested at the lab for me son, have my food tested for me dun, I 'm sick I can't even speak my lips are white dun, I'm sick."

Bouma hugged Calm tightly as he whispered back in his ear, I got you, and I'll have it tested as soon as I leave here. I'll do it for Kema and Raul and Providence. The two conversed for hours about everything that they could possibly think of. Calm ordered Bouma to check on his studio to make sure the lights were still on as the payments and rent was coming out of his account every month along with his apartment. His family had kept his poetry and open mic businesses running in New York City and Brooklyn while he was locked away but no one had been to the studio except the pregnant girl who refused to help Providence in any way while they turned tricks. Bouma had been the first scheduled visit for the week, but since Calm had been granted visitations his visitor list had been booked for weeks full of family and friends who had not been to his studio since he had been placed in a psychiatric facility.

At the end of the visit the two cried, Bouma promised he would do the best he could to get him out of the psychiatric facility and promised that he would handle his payments with his quarter million-dollar settlement that Kema's family had given to him from Kema's lawsuit money. He promised that Calm would be out just in time for his upcoming Strike Rally against bankruptcy that he had scheduled to attend in Detroit that he would be hosting next month. Bouma promised Calm the biggest block party after his release and hugged him once more before his departure.

Bouma was connected to Vanguard Services and Aegis testing laboratory by a friend. The lab tech promised Bouma results within four days. When the results were in the lab tech indeed found a substance known as Anticoagulants and Hypocalcaemia in his food which are substances found in rat poison. The lab technician claimed that if these types of chemicals are indeed part of Calm's meals, then he could die over time and an undercover observation would be necessary to prevent his death. The lab technician offered to locate a nurse who would secretly closely monitor, test and replace his food every day. If things went well, he would be released and put through physical therapy in no time. Bouma watched the lab technician as he phoned a nurse at NYC Psych facility for help. He notified the nurse that a client could possibly be knocked off because of some secret information involving the police.

Bouma heard loud noises coming from Calms studio. Before he approached the door he walked around back and peaked through the window into the small studio room. His heart fell as he recognised Providence being pimped by two twins. One twin had a gun in their hand standing outside the door and in the hallway while the other stood in the hallway smoking a Garcia Vega. He watched as Providence turned tricks on a dog leash being forced to bark for a john while he made fun of her. The john pulled the leash tightly around her neck practically choking her and causing some fixation. Bouma knew that he could not do it alone but he vowed to get his crew together and assassinate those ruthless twins if it was the last thing that he does. He phoned a gangster from a barbershop in Brooklyn and requested assistance. Luckily a mobster at the barbershop knew the father of the twins from Ohio. The mobster and his crew called the police and had the house surrounded. The police bust through the door and as the twins reached for their guns the police fired shots killing the twins instantly freeing Providence and safely returning her home to her friends and family in Brooklyn and Bushwick. A week later Calm had been released from the psychiatric facility by a nurse who had nursed Calm back to his health with medicines and a private physician who found Calm safe to return back to society. Bouma was glad to know that he could kill two birds with one stone by returning Calm and Providence back to this safe world, but he couldn't stop now he had made plans to bring Calm and Providence back together by placing them back in the music world and what better way to do it then to offer them a tour ride with community to Detroit Michigan. With the city of Detroit approaching bankruptcy city gardens, parks, and open areas would need to be repaired. Bouma and his organisation had vowed to bring a crew of volunteers who were willing to get the job done to restore the city. Although Bouma knew he would be taking a chance he wanted Calm and Providence to mark their territory in the music industry and perhaps get back to the sounds of Detroit's most native booty bouncing beats and cartoonist voices.

# Chapter 7

The phones had been ringing off the hook for weeks for almost two months now as Providence's mum could not deal with the harassment. Reporters from everywhere wanted to be the first to have the story about DJ Lady Lucina who Secret Society members held as a sex slave for over a year, while the founder was being poisoned to death in psychiatric ward over false accusations that the police had his girlfriend murdered. The scandal had become so big that Providence had agreed to go on a show similar to 20/20 ABC news. Shaw had scheduled the interview with this investigative series who had wanted to make it a 5-day series which included Providence for a 60-minute interview on Monday, Calm for a 60-minute interview on Tuesday, Bouma with a 60-minute interview on Wednesday, the three of them including her family with a guest therapist on Thursday, and then more therapy on Friday. Providence's family had been devastated by the whole kidnapping event as they said in the interview, "They were sure that she was dead until one day her baby called her and reassured her that she was still alive."

Her mother stated during the interview, "My baby was still alive I knew there was a God, a God who loved me and wanted to ease my mind to keep me from worrying all my life about Providence."

The father stated, "My baby had just lost her fiancé, she was proud to say he was a virgin, daddy, he's a virgin, a man who will bring me no diseases. But now look at my baby! Men have raped her and damaged her. She was practically a virgin who was waiting for the right man. They ruined my baby."

Providence's family had been present during all five interviews, crying in each interview whether on stage or in the crowd.

The journalist/interviewer held no mercy on Providence as she began with her questions. Providence answered to the best of her ability, "I had slept with a total 200 maybe 300 men overall. About four men a night, most of them clean business-like men in the music industry who were looking to touch me, feel me, or watch me. Most of the time I was put on leashes and I was given dog food I sniffed poop and had a lot, I mean a lot of anal sex, which was my major turn on for men. I was humiliated, cold, spanked a lot and high off of cocaine. Most of the time I pretended to be super high so they would feel that I was addicted enough to the point where they would not inject me with heroine. I was always told heroine was a drug that you never kicked and you still needed to take as methadone. I'd seen a lot of people who were hooked on heroine, and the methadone made them look even worse when they were coming off the medicine," (she starts crying), "excuse me while I cry a little. Anyhow I slept on an old mattress the whole time I was in sex slavery, and one day my prayers had been answered. I thought it was the pregnant girl who had told the police, but come to find out it was Bouma who had discovered me. The pregnant girl who was giving blow jobs had no mercy on me, often she would come there hoping to make money. It shocked me to see that another woman could care less about my situation. It really hurt. It made me feel hopeless in this world, to watch her come and go in out of the studio without being held captive. I just prayed every day, and one day my prayers were answered, my family's prayers were answered, and Raul my dead fiancé's prayers were answered. Since the situation, I have done nothing but sleep and eat my way back to health. When I see men on television or on the street, I wonder if they are here to kidnap me, or are they gonna kill me? But I remember, it was not the men on the street it was the members of the secret society who had chauvinist views the whole time they were members. They hated my power and they hated the fact that I had been given charity money for the organisation as well as $9,000 dollars for myself. That's all ACE ever said was that they gave some black girl more money at a performance than a founder. Often Ace wanted to go and withdraw the money but claimed it was too risky and they could be traced by tampering with my account. That's all he claimed during my kidnapping, stating out loud, 'Why would channel 7 give you anything? It's a man's world. You're just a squirrel now; give me the next nut and the next butt hump hoe.' Then he would send me in to do the next trick. It was like he had been in some jealous rage and had been holding it in for years. He could not wait to kidnap me. So often I have to reassure myself that it is not men in general. I just need to remember that I am a woman and watch my actions around men."

The journalist proceeded to ask the next question, "Providence, are you going back to the secret society?"

Providence responded, "I believe it should be an all-male organisation, I mean, I am pretty sure that the twins were not the only ones with this view towards women. I just don't feel like it is secure for women at this point. Don't get me wrong, I love DJ'ing and I want to continue my career as Lady Lucina someday but I want to do it on my own. No more organisations for me."

The journalist continued, "What about Raul's death? I heard he was a handsome Cuban virgin who was loaded with cartel money. That's something to be happy and ashamed of; ashamed because he had violated the rules and was supporting and expanding a cartel that began with clients after his DJ performances. How do you feel about knowing that he had chosen to take your producer's girlfriend, the one who had assaulted you and spent time on Rikers, to a boxing match in Puerto Rico? How do you feel, knowing that she was wearing expensive diamonds and a fur, and she was carrying half a million dollars in cash aboard the plane?"

"How do I feel? Well, if you knew the charming Raul like I had known him, you'd know that his intentions weren't to hurt me or Calm with Kema; only to smooth things out with her jealousy so she would not rage or show her tail at the album release party. I am pretty sure he wanted to ease her mind and I am dead sure Raul reassured her that I was in love with him and wanted nothing to do with Calm."

"OK Last question; how was your life with Raul?"

"He was romantic and overprotective. I will never forget the day he flew me to Miami to visit We Love Colours. It was like, OK, wherever you wanna go; we can go anywhere. I named the place and we were at the airport in less than three hours. It was so romantic and spontaneous. I loved him, he took my mind off the world and work. He was wonderful. I don't think I will ever find another man that compares."

When the interview ended cries could be heard from the audience. The interviews were so emotional, Bouma responded to the journalist; "All I could think about was saving her. She was on a leash, sniffing poop and eating dog food when I found her and Calm was dying. His skin was pale, his eyes were bugged, like they had been sewn open."

Calm's response to the journalist, "No more secret Society for underground DJs! I just want to close the whole organisation and sign over my rights to whoever would like to buy me out."

On the fourth day of the interviews, the twins, Ace and Bishop's father had requested to come on the show to do a formal apology. He cried and stated during the interview: "I am really sorry, Providence, about your pain and suffering. I am so sorry that you had to go through this. Now my sons are dead. The twins had developed so much animosity after their mother was shot and killed in Ohio that they had become woman haters. I knew something was up with them, they were spending too much time at that studio. The whole time I had my suspicions I never followed them to the studio. I wanted to, but I ignored my intuition. Come to find out they were harbouring a sex slave! They were coming home with thousands of dollars at a time. Just pimping a girl who had profited from being a DJ more than they had."

The fifth day ended with lots of advice and treatment recommendations for all of the parties involved in the matter. It was an emotional time for everyone, but somehow they would manage to get through it along the way.

# Chapter 8

The community workers in NYC as well as Providence's family, Calm's family and Bouma had boarded the tour bus that was heading for a two-month stay at the Crowne Plaza. The community members would be attending several meetings about the upkeep of abandon and bankrupt Detroit, Michigan. A variety of different scandals had occurred which had resulted in Detroit's abandonment. The community workers for NYC had several focuses.

One, to save the community gardens through recruitments and encouragements of inner-city volunteers.

Second, to offer upkeep for abandoned parks and playgrounds, so that the children could feel free to play during a trying time. Bouma's plan was to recruit as many people worldwide as possible and make them aware of Detroit's special community problems.

Community workers of NYC developed strategies by hosting free block parties for 3 weeks in various parts of Detroit, from sun up to sundown! The block parties would be filled with pamphlets about things such as HIV awareness, sex abuse, domestic violence, teenage pregnancy, homelessness, drug usage and drug dealing. Bouma felt that if he made the community aware of ongoing problems, then they would understand the connection that it had to the future through children.

Third, he wanted to make them aware about the need for fresh produce and how local markets could vanish soon without local gardening. During the first three days the community workers of NYC circulated and located various areas in Detroit that would go abandoned. The community workers of NYC managed to tape a wide variety of different kinds of abandoned supermarkets, fruit markets, abandoned gardens, ruined playgrounds and open areas with high grasses and large open areas. Also areas with many usable abandoned houses. The community workers created a film and planned to show it at every block party in order to make the community aware of what was going on and why volunteering was so necessary.

The first steps were to advertise, expose, and recognise the reasons for the oncoming poverty. Bouma and the community workers felt that this should go on for three to four weeks before they continued with the second step of implementing the work that had been perceived as necessary in order to keep Detroit alive.

Bouma and the community workers were relieved that Calm and Providence specialised in the music field. That way they were sure that the community would be entertained at all times without fear of being charged money by the hour. Bouma had assigned and put Calm and Providence in charge of the entertainment. During every rally, block parties, and night event, the two were in charge of providing suitable music free of charge, as that was the equivalent to community gardening and volunteering for the workers, as well as Bouma. The night before the first annual block party, Calm fell into a deep sleep and began dreaming about Kema. His first vision of her was her long silky brown hair that was being wrapped, rung and twisted in a towel. He then closed the shampoo and began brushing her hair. Suddenly, she turned and looked at him with providence's face. She looked him in his eyes and said, "Take care of Providence and you will be happy, always. You will not regret being by her side." Suddenly Calm woke up in a cold sweat. He looked around the room. The clock read 10:15 p.m. He grabbed the phone and dialled Providence's extension to see if she was awake. She answered on the first ring.

Providence: "Hello?"

Calm: "I had the dream again about her hair, only this time it was your face and she was asking me to take care of you, forever. I had a dream about her again. What am I gonna do? How can I let go of what we had? She started all this. Everything I have she gave to me. I love her so much and I thought we would be together always. (Calm begins tearing and he begins to sob). Please bring her back, Providence, I want her back. I wanna wake up and take a shower with her. I wanna give her money but I can't (he sobs loudly). I wanna kiss her, I wanna hear her voice; her yells, her moans, but I can't I just can't. It hurts, everything hurts."

Providence: "Meet me in the lobby. I know a place where we can go to get our minds off of Raul and Kema. I have cousins in the city who own something like an Elks club, a members-only club, very organised with soul and club music. I am going to call them right now. Will you come with me, Calm?"

No answer.

Providence: "Calm, are you there?"

Calm: "Yes. (He wipes his eyes and nose and sniffles) I am gonna get dressed. Should I wear Versace, or Armani?"

Providence: "Yes, Calm, you should wear both Armani and Versace tonight for the ladies. I want you to talk to my uncle and get some advice about how to cope with the loss of Kema. My uncle and Aunt were just like you two and when she died in a car accident he struggled."

Calm: "Seriously he can help me with advice. Cool I am getting dressed; anything to feel better."

Providence: "Anything for us to feel better. Anyhow, my uncle invited me down to his club this week. He would love to see a friend with me. The two of you can talk and smoke some of that good ole Jamaican weed in a zigzag paper. He will help you release your stress."

Calm: "Should I grab a Vega wrap for that Jamaican weed?"

Providence: "Heck no! My uncle is from the old school, he doesn't believe in anything but a pipe or zigzag papers; but trust me all you will need is a zig zag to release your stress. So get dressed and get on some of that good smelling cologne and meet me down stairs in an hour. Just one hour Calm! Sometimes you act worse than a girl when getting dressed."

Calm and Providence swerved through the allies in a taxi. The streets were filled with steam that was evaporating into the air from sewers. Prostitutes could be seen walking the streets and dealers and residents could be heard bellowing Detroit's native booty bouncing beats in their cars. Providence took Calm on a 30-minute tour. As they cruised through the east side she showed Calm a part of her neighbourhood that she had visited every summer since she was 13 years old. She reminded him of her career and how it got started, and how she had created and enhanced Detroit's native booty bouncing beats. Calm noticed a hip-hop dude man mugging him from a Cadillac Escalade. The dude hopped out the car with his telephone, questioning Providence about bringing snoops through the neighbourhood. Providence had known Jimmy all her life, but that still did not stop him from questioning. He mean-mugged Calm and threatened to shoot as he claimed that Calm was the reason that Providence had been a sex slave. Calm apologised and reassured Jimmy that he was not a snoop and had ample connections in New York. All it took was one phone call and he could have several dudes from the neighbourhood come through right now. Jimmy didn't believe him as he watched Calm describe the location and name the street on the telephone. Within ten minutes two Mercedes Benzes pulled up near Providence and Jimmy's cars carrying machine guns and oozes. Calm wanted jimmy to recognise how powerful he was. He wanted to let him know that he should never call a guy from New York a punk. The two sat outside for ten minutes just staring at each other holding guns while Providence begged for peace. Finally the two agreed to let go of the incident and go on with the night. Providence and Calm hopped inside of the Mercedes and drove away. Suddenly Providence began to realise how much of a man Calm was. It only took one phone call for her to realise that Calm was really connected worldwide. Instantly she felt a connection and an attraction to him. The Benz smelled so clean and fresh like it was fresh off the lot. She looked Calm up and down as the two stepped out of the car and walked into the Elks 'members-only club'. Besides her uncle and the weed, Providence wanted to be his next choice to getting his mind off of Kema, and with two months of alone time she was sure she could.

The block parties had been filled with games and entertainment. Calm had kept his men nearby fearing the return of Jimmy's thugs. Factory workers from GM, Ford, and Chrysler, told their horrific riches to rags stories. Many feared the day their unemployment ended, with dread. During the rallies, Bouma stressed online schooling for factory workers who were lacking in education and felt that taking a low wage job was beneath them. "Take online courses and go back to school before your unemployment ends." he stated.

"Today, I want you to think of the effect that bankruptcy will have on our children in the future," he stated. "Right now Mayor Bill de Blasio is investing in the future and he believes that children are the future."

"Today, I am here to stress the importance of fresh produce. You see these buildings and stores have all been shut down, abandoned, or have been closed in approximately two months' time. Most workers have been fired without notice and have no way of taking care of themselves. You see these abandoned houses and areas are now being used for drug trafficking, and sex trafficking.

"This is no good for our children and we need help. Our children do not deserve to grow up in these types of environments, filled with sex and drugs. You see these abandoned playgrounds; you see how high the grass is? We need volunteers to mow the grass so the kids can play. We need volunteers to water the gardens so we can grow inexpensive fresh tomatoes, cucumbers, onions, lettuce, and other fruits and vegetables."

The three weeklong rallies had been publicised on Detroit's local stations, which had all encouraged many volunteers to sign up. For a month straight, volunteers from Detroit and community workers imported from NYC went to several areas in Detroit, replanted gardens, watered crops, mowed lawns, cleaned playgrounds, and located buyers for abandoned supermarkets. The month had been long and tiring, and Bouma had hoped that after his departure Detroit residents would continue to care about their diminishing neighbourhoods. During the two months, he hoped for the best and promised to keep in touch with those who had taken the time to help.

# Chapter 9

The police busted into Orlando's dollar store with warrants and dogs the day after Raul and Kema's deaths. Orlando was also being charged as an accessory to drug smuggling for transporting into JFK. Unfortunately, he knew nothing about Rosa's stash spot and had passed the lie detector test with flying colours. He had warned Rosa about briberies and the dangers that it involved, but she refused to listen. Somehow, word got out that the shipment of money had come from Orlando's basement. The police searched his dollar store top to bottom and found nothing but old woodchips and back stock of shipments which were only merchandise for the store. Although he knew that Rosa was an accessory, he protected her and stood by her side, giving her great compliments as a hard worker in his store. During trial, he stood by her side even though he knew that Raul could possibly be some type of drug dealer who was in need of a stash spot.

The testimonies were intense as the prosecuting attorney's insinuated and repeatedly played back a video tape of Rosa leaving the dollar store in the evening and heading to JFK with a duffle bag that she had placed onto the tarmac and allowed Raul to pick up and board with. But, in the end, the attorneys could not confirm that any money was inside of the bag and they could not confirm what, if anything, was in the bag she left for Raul. The police had searched for clues and traces of money inside the duffle bag, but it had been completely destroyed in the explosion.

When the verdict came back not guilty, he was relieved. During trial Orlando had begun to realise that he still needed help at the dollar store. He looked to Rosa's fine-looking attorney for advice about some legal matters regarding criminal activity in the store and how to best protect himself in case this kind of incident ever happened again, or the police ever decided to open a new investigation against him in regards to drug trafficking.

The two had gotten quite close during the trial and somehow he had managed to fall in love with the attorney and out of love with Rosa, who he had now begun to feel was beneath him and stood for nothing but drug smuggling. The attorney had changed his mind set about 'all work and no play' and had managed to squeeze dinner dates and phone conversations out of him. He was pleased and proud to be seen with her. He longed for and admired her dark African American skin and her teased, wavy hair. Her body was slender and relaxing as she stood 5 foot 8 weighing 155 pounds. Erika had been a public defender for two years, in the criminal division of New York City's courts. She had agreed to take Rosa's case when it was presented to her. She felt that if she could help Rosa beat the case it would help her gain popularity and viability as a private attorney someday. What started as legal advice had turned into a love affair. Erika and Orlando then began dating on their down time. The relationship began to develop after several coffee chats and phone conversations and discussions about Rosa's case.

Before they knew it, the two were spending evenings at restaurants and days making lunch for each other on their off days. Erika had encouraged Orlando to expand and hire several employees for his store. She had assisted him by connecting him to business advisors who in turn then created and developed architect maps and plans.

Within a year the advisors had helped Orlando expand and now develop three separate dollar stores near downtown J Street, with several employees revolving between them. The advisors had assisted Orlando with hiring the proper key holders and managers to run the stores. The advisors felt that it was a perfect opportunity for growth, and at the same time Orlando would be able to relax more and have more downtime at home.

One day Erika had made a surprise visit to Orlando's home in Flatbush. The two had been sexing for quite some time now. She left her home and placed a positive pregnancy test and some yogurt cups from Yoplait into her bag. The two had been seeing each other for over two years.

Orlando was surprised to see Erika in such a frantic state. She covered his eyes as she pulled out the positive pregnancy test. Orlando was shocked by the pregnancy results. For years Orlando felt that his sperm was bad and he was incapable of producing children. Today Erika had reassured that he was the man that he had always hoped to be, and the man who could give his parents the good news that a healthy grandchild would be coming into the world soon. He caressed and rubbed the woman whom he wanted to spend the rest of his life with, dreaming of a beautiful new house. Erika had become so relaxing to him. She reassured him that everything was okay in her calm tone. She allowed him to express his manhood and she listened to every bit of his struggles about being a business owner and a boring lover. Erika had reshaped Orlando and now they were having a baby soon. Orlando searched the TV guide for Godzilla Bride for wedding tips. He wanted to officially make Erika his new wife someday. Just he, his baby, and his new wife in her new privately owned firm, which he was saving to help her open.

Rosa was happy that she had the beat the case against her and managed to maintain the dollar store in Spanish Harlem. She had learned all her skills from Orlando who was now living a new life and having a baby of his own with the attorney who had helped her beat the case. Although she felt sad that he had pursued the attorney in place of her, at least he did not agree to testify against her. Anyhow, Rosa had fallen in love with an up-and-coming boxer from Spanish Harlem named Young. He would be fighting his very first fight as a lightweight boxer on Saturday and was bringing Rosa and her family along to the fight. The two had met after Raul's death. Raul had appointed Young to take over where he left off. He had given Young Rosa's information, in case something ever happened to him. After the plane crash Young had finished the job in Puerto Rico and gotten out the game. He moved to Spanish Harlem where he began to pursue his boxing career while working security in Rosa's dollar store in Spanish Harlem.

Young had promised to take care of the kids on Raul's block, and as promised, he loaded his yard with water bottles and soda's while the kids played soccer in the streets during the summer time. Three years after Raul's death, Rosa and Young decided to throw a block party in memory of both Raul and Kema. This idea for a block party had come after Young had informed Rosa about Raul's ex-fiancée named Providence, who had been placed in sex slavery for almost two years by some crazy secret society members. Rosa sat in her living room with her family and watched the pre-recorded interviews that Providence and Calm had given to the journalists. Rosa and her family dropped to their knees as they heard the disturbed testimonies about sex slavery. Rosa begged Young to locate Calm and Providence and invite them to DJ the block party. She wanted everyone to be together in memory of their two friends who had died.

    The block party had been filled with festivities. Young watched Providence, Calm and Rosa as they conversed and cried about their loved ones' deaths. Rosa held Providence and Calm's hand as she shook her head in sorrow, while the two explained their horrible situations about sex slavery and psych wards. She poured fresh lemonade and fruit punch as she told stories about her and Raul's childhoods over Cuban steak and potatoes. Rosa and her family insisted that the two stay overnight and tomorrow they could spend the day at the pool and attend a boxing match in the evening.

    Young would be facing his first opponent, Mayo, from Puerto Rico. Rosa had provided both Calm and Providence with clothing and tickets for the upcoming boxing match. She had taken the two shopping during the afternoon. The boxing arena was busy and loud, as sounds from family members could be heard speaking and rooting for their fighter. The crowd was full of beautiful Latino girls wearing big hooped, expensive silver or gold earrings, big gold necklaces, and thick bracelets. Brand new scoop neck crop tops of red white and blue were accented by belly chains around their stomachs, as they waved money in the air and shouted about who would be the next lightweight champion of the world.

The smell of Latino males, wearing clean and refreshing colognes filled the air and mixed with fruity smelling female perfumes. The men ogled their girlfriends' bodies, as they allowed them to take control and converse. Providence tried to stomach the smell of so many scented men in the room.

Suddenly, Providence became very anxious and overwhelmed by men shouting and whistling and waving money. Calm grabbed her and held her as he pretended to be her man. He wrapped his arms around her and kissed her softly on her cheek as he reminded her that men are not bad, it was just the crazy society members who had been bad. She calmed herself and relaxed. The more she relaxed the more she realised how much she needed Calm in her life. She looked into his eyes as she confessed to him how much she loved him and needed him. Calm pretended to ignore her emotional state as he cheered on Young, who won the fight with a knockout punch in the third round.

# Chapter 10

Providence's psychological symptoms had been similar to most female sex slaves. Her signs involved recurrent night terrors of her sex slavery. She could not deal with men who smelled like strong cologne, as most of her abusers were businessmen looking for quick blowjobs. Often she had trouble getting a good night's sleep and was terrified of walking out the door, always looking behind her when she walked to the car. The smallest things triggered her memory, placing her into a terrified trance.

She had been in therapy for over a year and was terrified of going into a music studio. Part of her therapy was getting her back to who she once was. Often symptoms of sex slavery involved believing that one was worthless, without a future, becoming less interested in current activities, and always having the fear of being kidnapped again. The therapist felt that Providence could have her future back if only she trusted some people in normal society again. The therapist had set up several intensive therapy sessions with her and Calm, and felt that this would be a good way to get back to normal.

During the sessions, Calm had revealed his true inner self. He felt that no one would ever take the place of Kema but felt that Providence was worth producing and marketing. He felt just as scared as Providence about being back involved with the music industry. He felt scared for her and himself, as he did not know what the other society members were thinking, which worried him about a retaliation. Calm and Providence revealed their innermost fears. Providence was terrified of being run up on in a car, and terrified that she would be raped in public bathrooms. Calm was scared of being sprayed on the streets by a society member and scared of a sex partner cutting his throat while sleeping in his bed. The two had not had sex for years as they spilled their guts out in the intensive therapy sessions. Finally the therapist had made a suggestion that was obvious to all. Since the two were so worried about other people why not pursue a relationship with each other. Maybe the two of them could move in together and perhaps take care of one another. Perhaps they could even fall in love again and cry, make love, cook dinner, wash clothes and watch each other's backs.

Perhaps they could even produce music, slowly but surely, in the house together.

"Do what you have to do to become who you were all over again." The therapist suggested. "You were a producer Calm, and you were an artist Providence, who created music. Visualise your first performance and think about how nice and relaxing it was."

The therapist requested for the next session, "I want you to bring pictures of your photo shoots and performances. Bring the best pictures of yourself."

The next day, Calm and Providence attended the session. They placed all the photos of themselves onto the table. The therapist examined the photos carefully. Providence and Calm's photos had also been placed in a magazine for an upcoming album release party that the two had scheduled years ago.

"I see in these pictures of you, Providence, that you're colourful and energetic, full of spirit. Calm, you're so handsome and well groomed, like a savvy producer who's ready to produce upcoming artists. You two belong in the music industry in New York City. Now, remember, the music industry goes well beyond New York City. It goes to London, Tokyo, Sydney, Berlin, etc. These people would love to see you. They would love to know Providence and Calm's talents. The music industry is calling you. Music can be such a therapeutic release. Take all of your problems and stresses and put them into your music. Make a better CD than before, a hit maker that is guaranteed to top the charts. Remember, those fresh Detroit native booty-bouncing beats are still in you. You're still a good DJ Providence and you can get back to normal. You can get back to normal; you can be sexy and sure of yourself. And you, Calm; Kema is never coming back but she will always be with you in spirit. Give Providence a chance and let her be the good woman that she is. You're the only one she likes and is comfortable with. You're the only one. Be there for her, guide her, have studio time, invite your parents. Hire a bodyguard if you need to, encourage family members to sit in the loft with you. Develop an entourage full of family and people who you can trust. I know it's hard, but those men who put you into sex slavery were men who despised and had it in for you the whole time. They despised the fact that you were given money and assistance from the news stations. You were given $9,000 dollars during your first performance! Most DJs have to work six months before they see that amount. Those men had it in for you, they had sick minds and thoughts about putting a girl in sex slavery, simply because she was a woman who got a break. Trust me, all men are not bad. Most men don't want to kidnap you or torture you, they want to appreciate you and watch you prosper. Those twins, Ace and Bishop, were lucky to get shot. Imagine what would have happened to them if they had to show their faces around here now? The community would do worse than shoot them.

"Okay, before these last two sessions end and before you decide to go back into the world again, we have the test results and the blood works that you two agreed to take in regards to you pursuing new relationships, whether it be together or apart. So first, I would like to thank you for perfect attendance to therapy and I believe that you two will do well on your own. I want to thank you for your patience with me and your trust in my advice. I know it's not easy to believe in people at this moment, but somehow you managed to come here and participate. Now remember, I have office numbers and contacts in case you feel the need for more therapy. I am available 24 hours. Here is my cell number in case of an emergency. Feel free to contact my male assistant if necessary. OK so before we end this session, the two of you agreed to show me physicals to verify that you are in good health. Providence you have not received a physical since you were let out of sex slavery because you wanted to wait and see if you were possibly HIV positive. And Calm you wanted to wait and get a physical again to verify that you were in good health. So, Calm, you look pretty anxious, so we will start with your results first.

"First of all, your results state that you do carry the sickle cell trait. Next, your cranial and nerves appear to look normal so that means your mental health has definitely improved compared to the MRI from before. I recommend a small dose of medicine at night to prevent you from relapsing or developing bipolar disorder. I do see signs of rectal damage and liver damage so I recommend that you cut back on 300-dollar bottles of whisky and calm your nerves. Your heart looks good and your respiratory is average, could be better. But, other than that, no problems discovered. No venereal diseases or HIV.

"Now here is the good news for you, Providence. You are not HIV positive. You're not HIV positive, you're HIV negative and you definitely have something to live for. You have no further problems no cervical issues. You and Calm are good to go back into the world and live your lives. Remember the music industry needs you and they shouldn't have to live without you. Now give me a kiss on my cheek and we can go on with our lives."

Calm and Providence thanked the therapist for her intensive help and, now that they had completed their sessions, they were ready to return to the music industry as DJ Lady Lucina and DJ Calm.

# Chapter 11

Bouma loaded the tables with HIV pamphlets. Today he would be hosting an event for a Criminal Defence Attorney named Erika Hamilton who had recently opened up a new law firm. Erika had just recently gotten married and given birth to twins named Hudson and Alexandria. The public defender had opened a firm of her own so she could spend more time with her new twin babies. Unfortunately, business had been kind of slow since she began working for herself. Rosa had recommended that Erika hire Bouma to host a rally on her behalf, in order to bring in new clients. Bouma was good for organising rally events for upcoming attorneys who were in need of clients. Bouma had developed a plan and strategy to attract clients today. He had done some flyering around New York City and Brooklyn. The flyer read "Are you a client who is on the run and scared of facing severe charges during prosecution? Contact the office of Erika Hamilton. She will hear your testimonies and review your case free of charge and give you the best possible advice. Payments start when you make your first appearance in court". Bouma passed out flyers for the rally entitled "Scared Straight" for victims who were too scared to appear in court. The rally was a strategy to help Erika gain publicity. During the rally, Bouma selected two ex-criminals who had been on the run and found an attorney who cared. After several examinations of their cases, the two had their potential prison times shortened by about half. Bouma announced that any fugitive who was on the run and facing criminal charges could have their cases be examined and an approximation of the time they're facing, versus the time.

Erika could negotiate for in the courts, would be discussed free of charge. The rally was filled with criminals who were facing serious time because they had missed court dates and judges had issued bench warrants. Orlando, Erika, and some of her hired assistants examined various cases and discussed several possible negotiations. Before the rally had ended, Erika had 30 to 40 fugitives who were facing minor to moderate charges due to current warrants. Thankfully, the inmates trusted her judgment as they agreed to make down payments of $2,500 to $3,500 dollars each. Erika was running a special that required a one-time fee of $2,500 to $3,500 dollars flat for a retainer for representation and negotiations for lower sentencing if they pleaded guilty to their charges. She had negotiated with the courts, as she promised, to bring in 15 inmates each month who were willing to turn themselves in in exchange for better sentencing.

The inmates first discussed their negotiations for sentencing with Erika and her assistants. If they were satisfied with the negotiations, they were instructed to fill out the paper work out and sit in the back of the rally until the van departed to Rikers Island. Erika watched as the list filled up with suspects who had warrants. At the end of the rally, she loaded the criminals onto the bus and did a head count once more. She notified Rikers Island, giving them a list of suspects who were coming in tonight to prepare their warrants. The list read

Important Documents: Erika Hamilton's list of suspects and fugitives with warrants who are seeking negotiations to lower their sentencing in exchange for turning themselves in at Rikers Island during Erika's rally.

Providence had begun to get back to normal after her extensive therapy sessions. After therapy, she began to respond to strangers who wanted interviews and advertisements, eager to cash in on her fame and her story. Her first interview included a photo shoot with a wealthy breast cancer sponsor, entitled; "We are humans too".

The subsequent billboard was a symbolic portrait of various women from all different cultures, who come together to make a difference in the world regarding violence against women and sexual assaults. The billboard had been publicised all around the entire world as the organisation had endorsed Providence as one of their spokespersons. During a seminar session sponsored by the breast cancer association Providence had been chosen to attend. During her speech, her spirits had been dampened by a hate group who were attending. During the speech a member from the hate group yelled out; "How can you speak and open your mouth to people? Don't you feel like a prostitute? I mean I recognise you as a victim, but I can't help but wonder how many men have been inside you and I bet that you can't help but think it, too. I know you think in the back of your mind; are people disgusted to hold conversations with me because of ejaculations in my mouth?" Suddenly a woman in the crowd throws a hard saddle shoe and hits him on his shoulder. The whole seminar becomes a riot, and hurtful words begin to fly back and forth. After the seminar, Providence began to think that maybe she had been naïve not to consider how people viewed sex slaves. Yes, they felt sorry for sex slavery and people in it, but the reality is that perhaps sex slaves were viewed as dirty creatures that could never get their purity back, no matter how much they tried. Perhaps 10 years of celibacy could erase all the memories of sex and penetration. Providence decided to use a strategic approach to ease the crowd's thoughts during every seminar.

At the beginning of every talk that she gave, she would first start her speech by saying; "No matter what I do, I can never get my purity back. I will always be dirty and distasteful to some people, but I am just happy to be a survivor. I am happy that I escaped such tragedy. All I ask is that you love me for me. Learn from me to love and appreciate your life and freedom."

Providence decided to use the speech as an introduction during each seminar, because she needed to remain endorsed under her $100,000 each year endorsement contract. Besides the breast cancer awareness and violence against women campaign, Providence had received a few other endorsements in the advertising sector from NYC Hair Magazine with a hair model named Shaw and Planned Parenthood across the five boroughs.

Within months Shaw had turned Providence into a hair icon, placing her in magazine after magazine. She encouraged Providence to participate and work with NYC hair and often she used encouraging words like "Providence, it only takes one day out of the month to get paid. Now come on, perk up and let's get the hair and makeup done and the photo shoot in place."

Shaw had helped release Providence from her inner fears and had encouraged her to hit the club scene again on the upper east side. Providence rushed to her last seminar for the month at Planned Parenthood in Manhattan, New York. Today she would speak with HIV positive girls, who would be finding out their test results for the first time.

Most girls who are unable to cope, and request counselling and other assistance coping with the results, would be referred to Providence and other counsellors and volunteers. As part of training, the first thing that a speaker and counsellor must understand is that every client's situation is unique, whether they are HIV positive or not. Some patients are HIV positive from sharing needles and others are positive from sexual contact. Providence grabbed her chart and diagram as she waited for the first patient to enter. She was stunned to see that the first patient was the always a pregnant girl from the studio, who was giving blowjobs and had left her for dead. Tears started to form as the pregnant girl entered the room.

Providence: (Providence whispers to the patient) "You left me for dead in that studio room. You left me for dead!"

Pregnant Girl: "I didn't wanna get involved. I'm sorry but Ace and Bishop; they were my pimps too. You think I chose this profession? They were my pimps too. They pimped me every day for months at time. He swore to me that if I ever uttered a sound about you being kidnapped that he would kill me, my baby, my family, and my man. I knew he meant it and I couldn't chance it, I am sorry. I couldn't chance it. Even during the testimonies, I was still scared after they were dead. To this day, I am scared when I walk outside, thinking one of his boys is gonna get me and smoke me!"

Providence: "Me too. I just recently stepped out to a nightclub after almost three years now. I am having nightmares. I believe someone is gonna kill me, too. Those twins reminded me of twin demons, like it was the devil prophecy or some kind of rapture. The situation happened so abruptly I still can't believe it's me. If it wasn't for extensive therapy and all this assistance, such as support groups, I would probably commit suicide.

"But they helped me to remain strong, even stronger than before."

Pregnant Girl: "How is DJ Calm? I heard he went crazy. He was a suave, handsome dude that everybody wanted. But I heard Kema's death took a toll on him and he ain't been right ever since. Can you believe Kema drove him crazy? All that money, I bet he still got money! I bet he still rolling in the dough, crazy and all. Have you seen or heard from him?"

Providence: "No. After therapy we both went our separate ways. He had a few plans and project proposals and I started receiving endorsements. I have three different contracts right now and that's how I survive."

Pregnant: "So what about music? No more making music? I bet you're scared of any studios right now."

Providence: "Well, I'm taking it easy right now. Everything is just one day at a time. I feel a little shameful to flaunt my body, but I can hide it all behind the DJ booth. So what about you?"

Pregnant: "I got HIV from a John, my baby daddy is going to shoot me if he's positive. He left me and took custody of all my kids. Right now I am fighting legal battles trying to get visits. The judge ordered me to attend several group therapies before I can even get near them. You know that hurts, but I am getting through it. So about my results, I need medicine being that I am in the early stages. I can sustain it and still do my thing. The obstacle now is making sure my baby father is

HIV negative. Once he comes up negative, then I will be able to relax."

Providence: "What makes you think he's gonna come up negative? You two have a child together; that means there is a high chance of him being infected with the virus."

Pregnant Girl: "Yeah, but I just hope for the best. I just hope that my kids aren't infected at this point. It hurts to know that I have ruined my life and the life of someone who loves me, but I can't take back the past only work towards the future. And the future is seeking help to control the virus."

Providence: "Well here are the pamphlets and lists of centres that offer free assistance for HIV positive clients. You'll wanna call and schedule your own appointment. Remember to take your test results and they will handle everything from there."

Pregnant: "You know I wanna end up like you, helping people cope with reality. I mean, you've been through so much but yet you're still a helper. You are remarkable! (She hugs Providence). Listen, thanks for your help." (She grabs the information and leaves the room). Providence smiles as the pregnant girl departs. Although she wanted to offer her a place to stay, she could not find it in her heart to ever trust her again.

# Chapter 12

Rosa phoned Providence to invite her to Young's upcoming fight event in Brooklyn against his new opponent Del Rosa. Young had won three fights during the year and was said to probably end his winning streak tonight. It was said that Del Rosa has one of the toughest knock out punches that no one can recover from. He has been said to have given brain damage to most of his opponents. Young's trainer had taught him to stick and move quickly and swiftly. It was important that he understand how lethal Del Rosa's punches were. One wrong move and he could end up with a knock out and permanent brain damage. Young's family and Rosa's family argued with him not to go through with the fight. There were other fighters that he could choose to fight. So many people had passed on the opportunity to fight Del Rosa, why was he so different? Young believed that it was his destiny to go through with the fight. He had too much pride to decline any offer. He knew that he was taking a chance by agreeing to fight Del Rosa, but he went through with it anyway, because that is the only way to become champion. Young's coach trained him on running down the clock. Run down the clock, land punches and move swiftly. Do not go toe to toe with him unless you're sure he's shaken. Keep him in your eyesight and don't let him sting you. His punches sneak up on you and they can have a sudden effect, so be careful. Rosa knew that this could possibly be the last time that Young participated in a fight, so she phoned everybody to notify them of the possibility that Young could become permanently brain damaged and could possibly never fight again. Regardless, Providence was excited to attend. She purchased her ticket online and used her promo code that Rosa had given to her for front row tickets. Rosa arrived at the fight 30 minutes before show time. Again, the smell of fruity smelling perfumes, male colognes, and loud sounds filled the air. Money was waving everywhere, boos and laughters could be heard as people voiced opinions on Young and Del Rosa.

Providence was surprised when DJ Calm walked into the room. He was looking better than ever! Things had definitely gotten back to normal for him. She looked him in his eyes for the first time in over a year. Suddenly she felt a rush of love come over her, as though she and Calm had been broken apart and had managed to get back together again. She tried to hide her feelings as he approached her. She pretended to yell and cheer. Rosa and her family were crying as they pleaded with Young not to go through with the fight. Money had been put in the air and bribes had been offered in order to protect Young from his monster opponent.

An 8,000-dollar offer had been placed on the table, then added to, for whichever opponent agreed to withdraw from the fight. The bid went once, the bid went twice, and then suddenly someone grabbed all the money placed on the table and this ended the fight. The amount of money in total was $13,000 dollars, just to walk away from the fight.

The families cheered as they were both happy and satisfied. One side of the room was happy that Del Rosa would remain the lightweight champion of the year and the other side of the room was happy to know that Young had come to his senses in his amateur boxing career.

Most of the crowd felt that it was too early in Young's career to fight such a seasoned boxer with such power. "Give it a couple of years," his coach yelled. "The best talent in boxing is knowing when to give; knowing when something is not right and when you're not ready. If I did not care for you, I would not be telling you this, but you're not ready. Take the money and live to fight another day." Young's coach smiled at him as the fight was ended and he gladly threw in the towel. Young glanced at Rosa and watched her reaction as she smiled and screamed approval. Young was happy he had listened to his friends, family, and coaches, but he was worried about reimbursements so he made an announcement on stage to those who felt unsatisfied with his decision not to go through with the fight can be reimbursed on the spot. Out of the 86 people who attended the fight only 5 people requested their money back. The rest were mostly family members and friends, happy that it had been cancelled.

After the fight cancellation, Calm was waiting outside for Providence in a black Cadillac Escalade. He wanted to cruise Manhattan and listen to Aaliyah while he reminisced about the past with Providence. He could not help but lust after her, especially after seeing her restored slender curves on billboards everywhere. It had been a year since the two spoke and he truly missed her. Calm grabbed Providence and held her arm asking her if she had any plans after the event. Suddenly Rosa ordered everybody to go to Raul's restaurant on the upper East side for food and drinks. The restaurant was closed for Young's so-called after party. Calm grabbed Providence and offered her a ride to the restaurant. Providence happily climbed into the backseat with Calm. He told the driver to put on Aaliyah as he smiled at Providence seductively. Providence sensed that this was finally her chance to be with Calm. She tongue-kissed him for several minutes before coming up for air. The two had missed each other over the years that they had spent apart, and suddenly realised how much they meant to one another. Providence responded sarcastically and shamefully as she looked in to his eyes and whispered, "Have you ever kissed a prostitute before so passionately?" Calm responded by saying, "Yes, last time I kissed you." He smiled softly. "Kema had so many men before me from Staten Island and Queens, she was never settled before me and I don't believe she would have been settled after me and yet I loved her, you know. I mean she was my everything. I just want to start fresh and I believe that I want to spend the rest of my life with you. Whether you were a prostitute or not, I want to spend my life with you. Let's make music again, Providence, let's just start again."

"You promise you won't use my past against me; do you promise?"

"Yes, I promise. We can just look to the future and pick up where we left off. We can take it slow and build a life together."

Providence and Calm arrived at Raul's restaurant on the upper East side. The restaurant was filled to capacity with people from the cancelled boxing match. Providence and Calm squeezed through the crowd as they made their way to the bar. Latino, R&B, and hip-hop music filled the room along with laughter and smiles from the crowd. Providence and calm ordered some Don Julio tequila-filled nachos with jalapenos which the bartender had recommend that they order it if they wanted to feel slightly drunk and happy. The happy tequila nachos he called them.

The crowd was going wild. Providence and Calm watched as Young strolled through the restaurant like a celebrity. Women were all over him kissing him on the cheek, hugging, him and giving him their numbers. Men congratulated him as they wrote down the number to his campaign and promised to donate money for his next fight purse.

Providence never realised how wealthy the Latino community was. The men appeared so rich and macho as they accommodated Young with donations and ordered food for families of ten or more at a time. Gold-flooded most of their necks and their babies walked around with finger rings of Puerto Rican gold. Older mothers in their late thirties, looked fine even though they had recently had baby number five or higher. Calm conversed with Providence about the Latino community and how wealthy the families were.

He discussed the importance of manhood for men and the importance of childbearing for women, and how they played key roles in relationships. As the night began to progress, the restaurant had become filled to almost capacity. Young had an announcement to make and he got everyone's attention. He was holding a small velour box that looked to have a ring inside of it. Once he got everyone's attention, he requested that Rosa join him for his announcement. First he announced that he had been offered a new challenger and would be accepting the offer to fight another lightweight boxer from Mexico in a couple of weeks. Next he wanted to thank the audience for all their support over the years. He was happy to announce that he would be organizing an entourage soon and anyone interested in joining the entourage could sign up to be a member.

After the announcements were made, Young asked the DJ to please cut the music while he made his last and final announcement. He grabbed the microphone and bent down on one knee. He then looked at Rosa and began to speak to her.

"How selfish I was not to notice the tears in your eyes Rosa. I could have lost my life. I did not consider how you felt or how anyone else felt about fighting out of my league and Del Rosa's knockout punch. I was not ready to challenge him. I promise baby that I will never do that again. I will take your advice very seriously. What a woman you are for putting up with me because of my stupid and selfish decisions. I don't know what I was thinking but honestly, I was not fully aware of the consequences."

"And then suddenly it hit me! I thought to myself, *Are you crazy?* I looked around the room and I saw tears in everyone's eyes, and that's when I realised that I was pushing it, so I called it off and I grabbed the thirteen thousand dollars off the table."

"I wanna tell you that you are any man's 'dream come true.' You are beautiful, sexy, compassionate, caring, and understanding. You are what every man needs in his life and I don't think that I can go another day without you. You know, I promised to take over where Raul left off when he left me instructions to take care of Rosa and her family. I knew it would be a task but now I thank god for meeting you and I just can't go another day without asking you being my wife. Rosa, will you marry me?"

(Oohs and aahs can be heard from the crowd).

"Yes Young, I will marry you."

"Then it is official! You are gonna be my wife and make me the happiest man on earth."

The night was filled with love laughter and hope. Hope of love between Calm and Providence, hope between Young and Rosa, and hope that Young would defeat his next opponent from Mexico in the newly scheduled fight in two weeks. Providence admired Rosa as she would become the wife of a young boxer. Deep down inside she hoped that Calm offered to marry her and, with this new opportunity, to create a better understanding between the two of them. She felt that their chances were high. But, who knows? Only time would tell. Who could tell what the future holds? But Providence knew right now that she would make love endlessly to DJ Calm.

A year later Providence and Calm opened up a practice known as 31 Platinum Grills. The practice was developed, created, and sponsored by Bouma, the Jewellery Store Owner. The business specialised in designing mouth fronts with gold or platinum grills for celebrities and other customers who wanted beautiful and expensive mouth fronts. Providence continued to accept endorsements and work as a speaker for violence against women. Calm eventually became a music producer and even produced Providence's first underground album filled with 'Detroit's Native Booty Bouncing Beats'. Although Providence made no real live appearances, her CD had topped the charts as one of the best underground albums of the year. Rosa and Young got married in Vegas and a year later he became the undefeated champion of the world. Orlando and Erika are married with two children and are running an intensely busy law firm, thanks to the help of Bouma.

Bouma continues to be an organiser and activist and is currently holding a campaign for youth that rallies against suicide.

The always pregnant girl from the music studio is still living with HIV. Her baby father is also living with HIV and the two have gotten back together and are raising their children, who have no trace of the virus.

Remember everybody needs somebody in this world, and nobody should have to live alone.

Peace from Pyjama Stories Volume 2, the Secret Society of 31 Platinum Grills.

# Author's Biography

Tanea Hill is a 35-year-old woman raised from a single parent household with an overseas military background. She was born in Frankfurt, West Germany, but was raised by a legal guardian, off and on, and resided in Ypsilanti Michigan most of her life.

As a military child she travelled the world from Germany to France to California to New York. She even watched the turn of events when the East Berlin wall came down, after she had just visited it one week prior, on a field trip with her schoolteacher.

Such experiences with travel were common, throughout her life, leading to her fascinations with creative arts; such as dancing, music writing, poetry, book writing and script writing.

Tanea is currently attending Brooklyn College and working towards her Master's Degree in Sociology. Her major has assisted her with book writing, helping her to write real-life books with real-life events about race, class, gender and social change.